KU-516-687

NOT HEARERS ONLY

NOT HEARERS ONLY

Bible Studies in the Epistle of James

JOHN BLANCHARD

WORD BOOKS
LONDON
and Waco, Texas, U.S.A.

Published by Word Books, London,
a Division of Word (UK) Ltd, Park Lane,
Hemel Hempstead, Hertfordshire.

ISBN 0 85009 032 6

Printed and bound in England by
Hazell Watson & Viney Ltd,
Aylesbury, Bucks

TO JOYCE

FOREWORD

All who have heard John Blanchard speak will be delighted to know of this series of studies in the Epistle of James. Mr Blanchard is one of the most able of the younger generation of new preachers who are rapidly coming to the fore. His ministry in evangelistic crusades, at the great Holiday Crusade at Filey, and in the holiday house-parties arranged by the Movement for World Evangelization has always been widely appreciated by all ages. Those who know his ministry will not be disappointed with this book. It reflects Mr Blanchard's ability to set out clearly the gist of a passage of scripture, combined with the rare gift of making it apply to life as we all know it. There is the refreshing wealth of illustration which comes from a wide range of reading and which many workers will find useful to draw on for their own work. The whole book is easy to read and yet challenging to put into practice. This book merits a very wide circulation and we trust will be a source of inspiration to thousands of Christians who may or who may not have had the privilege of sitting under John Blanchard's ministry.

GEORGE B. DUNCAN

PREFACE

The Epistle of James has always had a peculiar fascination for me, ever since I first 'discovered' it soon after my conversion. From then on I have been drawn to it again and again. It was one of the first parts of the Bible I went through as a Bible Class leader at Holy Trinity Church, Guernsey in 1958, using, I remember, Canon Guy King's book *A Belief that Behaves* as a general basis. Later, when I travelled to England as a member of a parish mission team, the Vicar of the Church involved based his daily ministry to the team on the same Epistle, and I began to gain new insights into this great little book.

Some years afterwards, as a staff evangelist with the National Young Life Campaign, I dug a little deeper as I studied it in series with several NYLC branches in the West Country. Then in 1966, on the staff of the Movement for World Evangelization, I led the first of what has since become a large number of delightfully happy house-parties in Europe and elsewhere. Yet again I felt irresistibly drawn to the Epistle of James as a basis for the morning Bible Hour, and I found myself returning to the text with a new enthusiasm to discover fresh truths from the familiar words.

In the Autumn of 1968 I accepted an invitation to write a series of Bible Studies for 'Sunday Companion', and found great joy in re-shaping material on the first chapter of James to meet the particular demands of 1,000-word articles for 29 weeks. Those articles, later translated for use in Eastern Europe, greatly added to requests I was already receiving to consider producing a devotional study on the whole Epistle of James in more permanent form. This book is the beginning of the answer.

Anyone even vaguely familiar with the New Testament knows the general line of the Epistle of James, and a glance at some of the titles of books devoted to it confirms the assessment that is made—*The Behavior of Belief* (Spiros Zodhiates). *A Belief that Behaves* (Guy H. King), *Make Your Faith* Work (Louis H. Evans), *Faith that Works* (John L. Bird), *The Tests of Faith* (J. Alec Motyer). These titles are all trying to crystallize the same truth, that James is a *practical* book, dealing with everyday life for the man in the street. Yet it is not devoid of doctrine, as we shall see when we begin to dig into the text. As Alec Motyer puts it, '. . . the distinctive value of James is his striking grasp of the integration of truth and life'. I agree!—and it is precisely this integration of truth and life that makes James so relevant today. Even as Christians we seem to have an almost incurable tendency to be unbalanced. We either major on accumulating truth, to the neglect of enthusiastic action, or we dash around in a mad whirl of activity, to the neglect of faith and truth. James provides just the balance we need. It is said that when a student was once asked to name his favourite translation of the Bible he replied 'My mother's.' 'Is it a translation into English?', his friend went on. 'No', he replied, 'it is a translation into action!' That, in a nutshell, is James's great concern.

In these studies, I have not sought to deal with critical and technical issues, which are beyond both my aim and my ability. I have therefore assumed, for instance, that the writer of the Epistle was 'James, the Lord's brother'

(Galatians 1:19) and that is was written at some time between A.D. 45 and A.D. 62. I have simply come to the Word of God with an open heart and sought the Holy Spirit's help in understanding and applying it. In preparing these studies for publication in this form, I have sought, by use of the second person, to retain as much as possible of the personal thrust of the spoken word.

I would like to express my thanks to the Council of the Movement for World Evangelization for the privilege of serving the Movement in the ministry of the Word of God, to Word (UK) Limited for their kind offer to publish these studies, to the Rev. George B. Duncan for his gracious Foreword, and to Miss Sheila Hellberg for her great patience in typing and re-typing the manuscript to meet the demands of an author who never quite seemed to be satisfied!

May the Lord help writer and reader alike to obey His own clear command, given through James, to be 'doers of the word, and *not hearers only*'!

Weston-super-Mare,
Somerset.
September 1971

JOHN BLANCHARD

CONTENTS

Chapter 1

TO GOD THE GLORY

> *'James, a servant of God and of the Lord Jesus Christ, to the twelve tribes which are scattered abroad, greeting.'* (James 1:1)

In modern practice, this verse would represent no more than the 'Dear Sir' and 'Yours faithfully' of a letter, together with the signature of the sender—yet there is a wealth of deep spiritual truth locked into these words.

One way of discovering the riches we have here is to see the verse as saying three important things about the man who wrote it.

Firstly, he had *a lowly consideration of himself*—he calls himself 'James, a servant'; secondly, he had *a lofty conception of his Saviour*—he says he is a servant of 'God and the Lord Jesus Christ'; thirdly, he had *a loving concern for the saints*—he writes to 'the twelve tribes which are scattered abroad, greeting'. There is so much truth in these three statements that we must look at them carefully in turn.

1. *A lowly consideration of himself.*—'James, a Servant'.

If this Epistle had been cut short after the first three words, we would know that we were looking at the beginning of an unusual book, written by an unusual man, for having given us his name (which he must do in order to identify the writer in the first place) the very next thing he says about himself is just about the lowest thing he could possibly say! Just think of some of the things he could have called himself. He could have written 'James, an Apostle'. He could have written 'James, the leader of the Church at Jerusalem' (in Acts 21:18 Luke reports that 'Paul went in with us unto James; and all the elders were present'). He could have written 'James, a pillar of the Church' (in Galatians 2:9 Paul writes of 'James, Cephas, and John who seemed to be pillars'). Even more significantly, he could have begun his letter 'James, the brother of Jesus' (in Galatians 1:19 he is identified as 'James, the Lord's brother'). In either of the first two alternatives he would have been able to exalt himself, in the third he would have been able to bask in all the reflected glory of having been brought up, and lived together, and shared his young life in close personal touch with the Lord Jesus. It was perfectly true, of course, but it would also, in a very subtle way, have been a clever bit of one-upmanship over Peter and John and Matthew and Mark, and even over the mighty Paul!

Do you find an echo there of something that is very real in the heart of every one of us, if we are really honest?—and that is that by nature we are incurably inclined to get to ourselves every last iota of credit and glory and limelight that we possibly can. James could have used all kinds of names to get credit to himself—reflected credit, it is true, but even that is good enough for most of us!—instead of which he deliberately choose a phrase which literally means 'a bond slave'. The mark of a man of God is not that he thinks a lot of himself, but that he thinks very little of himself. As somebody once put it 'a great man never thinks he is great; a small man never thinks he is small'.

Have you ever noticed Paul's wonderful example of this in 1 Corinthians 3? The Christians at Corinth seemed to be making a lot of fuss over the two people whose ministries had been a means of such great blessing to them, Paul and Apollos. Having told them how wrong this sort of thing was (and *there* is a word for today!) he goes on—'who then is Paul, and who is Apollos, but ministers by whom ye believed, even as *the Lord gave to every man.* I have planted, Apollos watered; but God gave the increase. So then *neither is he that planteth anything, neither he that watereth; but God that giveth the increase*' (vv. 5–7). In effect, he is saying 'Forget about Paul, forget about Apollos. We are nothing. Give all the praise and glory to God, and to God alone!' In the same way, at the very moment when his ministry was being vindicated in the eyes of all the people, John the Baptist says 'He (the Lord Jesus) must increase, but I must decrease' (John 3:30).

A friend once told me of an African who had been comparing two missionaries working in his part of the country. 'One of them' he said 'was unselfish; but the other was selfless.' Do you see the difference? It is possible to be generous, hardworking, sacrificial and endlessly busy in the Lord's service, and yet to be eaten up with self. You may be doing things, sharing things, giving things—but are you deliberately putting yourself in the position where you will not be noticed, and where no credit whatever will be given to you? Kenneth Wuest once wrote 'The only Person who had the right to assert His rights waived them', and of course he was referring to the Lord Jesus,—especially to the way He is spoken of in that amazing passage in Philippians 2, where we read —'Let this mind be in you which was also in Christ Jesus; who, being in the form of God, thought it not robbery to be equal with God, but *made Himself of no reputation*'. I am afraid that those last five words can very seldom be said of the average Christian! We have proud hearts, all of us, and when that pride asserts itself it does so because we deliberately or ignorantly forget that of ourselves we have nothing of which we *can* be proud! To see ourselves in perspective, we need to remember at least two things:

Firstly, that we are owned by God. Writing to the Christians at Corinth, Paul says 'You are not your own; you were bought with a price' (1 Corinthians 6:19–20 RSV). Surely that helps to put all our service and sacrifice in its rightful place! In the ancient world, a servant was not somebody on a payroll, but somebody who was part of a master's property. A servant, or bond-slave, did not go around looking for a master, choosing one he liked, and then dictating the terms of his employment and grasping at credit for all he did. The master did the choosing, and paid the price, then sent the servant to work, and, as he owned him, had the right to expect loyal and humble obedience. Now link that with John 15:16, where Jesus says 'Ye have not chosen me, but I have chosen you, and ordained you, that ye should go forth and bring forth fruit. . . .' Writing from Cambridge in 1883, C. T. Studd said 'I had known about Jesus dying for me, but I had never understood that if He had died for me then I did not belong to myself. Redemption means buying back, so that if I belonged to Him, either I had to be a thief and keep what wasn't mine, or else I had to give up everything to God. When I came to see that Jesus Christ had died for me, it didn't seem hard to give up all for Him.' Remember, then, that you are owned by God.

Secondly, what we owe to God. Again in writing to the Corinthians, Paul asks 'What have you that you did not receive?' (1 Corinthians 4:7 RSV). Have you ever stopped to think that question through? It is a wonderful antidote to arrogance and a wonderful help to humility! Of course it is easy to begin a list of things you *do* owe to God—your life and liberty; your health and strength; your gifts and abilities; every virtue and victory; every faculty and power; every answered prayer; every forgiven sin; every source of joy; every hope of heaven. The list is endless. But the point of Paul's question becomes even clearer when you try to answer it the other way round. Try making a list of all the advantages, abilities, blessings and benefits you have and that were *not* given to you by the Lord! Do you see the point?

James had a lowly consideration of himself, and as a result his ministry and service were seen in exactly the right light. Because you are owned by the Lord and because of all you owe to Him, perhaps you ought quietly and thoughtfully to re-assess your opinion of yourself. Maybe these words by Frances Ridley Havergal will help you to do so:

Not your own, to Him you owe
All your life and all your love.
Live that ye His praise may show,
Who is yet all praise above.
Every day and every hour,
Every gift and every power,
Consecrate to Him alone,
Who hath claimed you for His own.

2. *A lofty conception of his Saviour.* James goes on to say that he is the servant 'of God and of the Lord Jesus Christ'.

Over 200 years ago, Isaac Watts wrote a wonderful hymn which began like this:

Join all the glorious names
Of wisdom love and power,
That ever mortals knew

That angels ever bore;
All are too mean,
To speak His worth,
Too mean to set my Saviour forth.

James would certainly have agreed with that!—for having as it were lowered himself in the eyes of his readers and made quite certain that as far as he was concerned all he would claim was to be a bond-slave, he then exalts the Person of His Saviour by giving Him 'a name which is above every name' (Philippians 2:9). Every Christian should make it his constant aim to exalt his Lord and Saviour, Jesus Christ—

Firstly, in his witness. A friend of mine, a young preacher, was once given some advice by a mature Christian of many years' experience, and I think it is the finest that could ever be given to any preacher in the world. It was this—'Young man, whenever you preach, be sure that you do two things—lift the Saviour high and lay the sinner low'. There is a great need for that kind of preaching today! Some preaching seems to run the risk first of all of suggesting that there are all sorts of things a sinner can do to make himself acceptable to the Saviour, and then of bringing the Lord down so low in order to make Him accessible to the sinner, that one is eventually presented with the invitation that two equals should come to an agreement. Beware of doing either of those two dangerous things! Lift the Saviour high and lay the sinner low! Let me just underline that, not only for preachers, but for all who share in the work and witness of the Church. Never make the mistake of thinking that evangelism consists of trying to tell people how miserable and unhappy and depressed and empty their lives are, and then that there is Someone called Jesus who can answer all their problems. Be sure to do more than that, in both directions; first of all by showing men that they are spiritually *dead*, and then by telling them not just what they must do but what Jesus has done, and, most important of all, who Jesus is! Then, like the Apostle Peter on the Day of Pentecost, be sure that you preach Him not only as 'Jesus' but also as 'both Lord and Christ' (Acts 2:36).

Secondly, in his worship. In the best sense, of course, this comes first and not second. So often our work and witness for God is powerless because our worship is so poor. So much is done in the energy of the flesh rather than in the ecstasy of our faith. And there is another, equally serious, possibility, and that is that we get so tied up with our programme that we lose sight of the wonder and the glory that surrounds the living Person of the Lord Jesus Christ. There is a vast and vital difference between reading the Bible every day to accumulate knowledge, and coming into the presence of the Lord Jesus and worshipping Him for what He is. Lift the Saviour high!

Perhaps I ought to carry that line of thought a little further. One of the great glories of evangelicalism is the doctrine of justification by faith, and by faith alone, on the grounds of the shed blood of the Lord Jesus in His finished work on the cross. But if that is one of evangelicalism's great glories, let me tell you one of its great dangers, and that is the danger of forgetting that although Christ's death on our behalf gives us liberty of access, it does not mean that we can have looseness in our approach. We *do* have 'boldness to enter into the holiest by the blood of Jesus' (Hebrews 10:19)—but we are not to allow boldness to become brashness! Make a note of that! Nothing saddens me more than to hear Christians—young Christians especially—giving the impression when they are praying that they are on 'buddy buddy' terms with God. Now it is wonderfully true that in John 15:15 Jesus said to His disciples, 'I have called you friends', but that does not alter the fact that He is 'King of Kings and Lord of Lords' (Revelation 19:16). Because we can focus on His humanity, let us never forget His Divinity. An advance in the Christian faith ought never to bring us to the position where we do not have a sense of awe and wonder in contemplating the Person of the Lord Jesus Christ. Justification does of course mean that we are right with God but it does not mean that we are equal with Him! Underline that! It is still true that His ways are higher than our ways and His thoughts than our thoughts. Lift the Saviour high!

Notice how high James lifts His Saviour! There was a time when he had not believed on Him at all—he would have been included in the indictment of John 7:5, '. . . neither did His brethren believe in Him'. Later, however, had come that glorious day when he had met with Jesus after His resurrection—the Holy Spirit guides Paul to tell us specifically that '. . . He was seen of James' (1 Corinthians 15:7). Now he describes Him (and the words in the text could be translated like this) as 'Jesus Christ, who is God and Lord'. Notice how perfectly that describes Him.

He is JESUS. The word means 'Saviour', and sums up His purpose in coming into the world. The angel's message to Joseph was 'Thou shalt call His Name Jesus, for He shall save His people from their sins' (Matthew 1:31).

He is CHRIST. This is the Hebrew word 'Messiah', or 'anointed One' and tells us not why Jesus came, but on

Whose authority! The Jewish people were oppressed by enemy occupying forces, and for 400 years (the period between the Old and New Testaments) there had been no sign of the Deliverer promised by God. Now He had come!

He is GOD. When Thomas met with the risen Jesus he cried 'My Lord and my God' (John 20:28) and the Christian's conception of Him should be nothing less than that of the Apostle Paul, that Christ is 'over all, God blessed for ever' (Romans 9:5).

He is LORD. Of course He is, if He is God! He is the Owner and Master of all His people, with the right to reign and rule in their hearts and lives. It was surely this conviction that gripped James as he wrote these opening words, giving him a lowly consideration of himself and a lofty conception of his Saviour. The last verse of that great hymn by Isaac Watts sums it up exactly:

My Saviour and my Lord,
My Conqueror and my King!
Thy sceptre and Thy sword,
Thy reign of grace I sing.
Thine is the power; behold I sit
In willing bonds before Thy feet.

3. *A loving concern for the saints.* James addresses his letter 'to the twelve tribes which are scattered abroad, greeting'.

Before I was converted, I used to hear one particular verse of Scripture read in church again and again—usually before the collection was taken!—and the verse was Galatians 6:10, 'Let us do good unto all men, especially unto them who are of the household of faith'. Being unconverted at the time, I felt perfectly able to pass judgment on the Bible, and I can well remember thinking that

that verse was a nasty bit of nonsense. Why, it turned Christianity into the worst kind of closed shop, a huddle of self-satisfied snobs looking after themselves very comfortably and caring nothing for the rest of the world. Of course you only have to read the first part of the verse carefully to see that my judgment was unfair. An unconverted person always has a warped judgment on spiritual issues, for the reason given by the Apostle Paul in 1 Corinthians 2:14—'But the natural man receiveth not the things of the Spirit of God; for they are foolishness unto him: neither can he know them, because they are spiritually discerned.' I had no idea at that time of the wonderful picture the Bible gives of all Christians being members of the same household and family, and therefore bound together not by their selfish choice of each other, but by the Lord's sovereign choice of them! When writing to the Ephesians, the Apostle Paul said that he had heard two things about them—'your faith in the Lord Jesus and your love toward all the saints' (Ephesians 1:15 RSV). Writing to the Colossians he says exactly the same thing, that he had heard of 'your faith in Christ Jesus and of the love which you have for all the saints' (Colossians 1:4 RSV). Faith in the Lord and love for the Lord's people went hand in glove in the New Testament, and they should still do so today!

James had it exactly right, for having told us of his faith in Christ, he demonstrates his concern for the welfare of his fellow Christians by sending them this letter of encouragement. However, that is anticipating the background of the people to whom he is writing! Let us look at what we are told about them. They are 'the twelve tribes which are scattered abroad'. I can never read those words without seeing two great truths, one terrible and one triumphant.

The first is the pressing hand of Satan—these people were 'scattered abroad'. In his little book on the Epistle of James, *Make your Faith Work*, Louis H. Evans says 'Those of the Dispersion were those in captivity, in slavery. Israel and Judah had been taken captive; they had been torn away from friends and country; they had suffered all the indignities of a conquered people. They were starving, homesick, the most loathed of men. Under the heel of the pagan conqueror, it would be natural for them to cry out 'Where is God?' James writes to tell them!' Many of those early Christians knew a great deal of the pressing hand of Satan. Ripped and rooted from their own familiar surroundings, they were now 'strangers scattered throughout Pontus, Galatia, Cappadocia, Asia and Bithynia' (1 Peter 1:1). Because of their faith, they lived under constant pressure. As we shall see more clearly later on, this is always a picture, and often a parallel, of the experience of all God's people in every age. Even those great heroes of the Old Testament 'confessed that they were strangers and pilgrims on the earth' (Hebrews 11:13). Let us be quite sure of this—the Christian should expect to meet with difficulties, trials, temptations, oppression, misunderstanding and rejection, to a greater or lesser degree. Anybody preaching that once a person becomes a Christian he has no more troubles and difficulties in this world, or that the Christian life is easy and undemanding, is preaching from an empty head and a closed Bible! Jesus said to his first disciples '. . . because you are not of the world, but I chose you out of the world, therefore the world hates you' (John 15:19 RSV). The persuasions and pressures of the world are all around the Christian, and are instruments in the pressing hand of Satan.

The second is the preserving hand of God. James calls

his readers 'the twelve tribes'. That little phrase seems to me to speak in a very wonderful way of the preserving hand of God around His own people. They may have been 'scattered abroad', but they were still 'twelve tribes'! They may have been split apart by satanic pressure, but they were still held together by Divine power! What a tremendous word that is for today! The Lord's people may be oppressed, they may be in trouble, they may find the going hard, they may be in a minority, they may be persecuted, they may be thought ill of, they may be misunderstood, they may be ridiculed, they may be thought irrelevant by the world—but they are still 'the twelve tribes', what Paul in Galatians 6:16 calls 'the Israel of God', held secure in His preserving hand. The Epistle of James does not seem to have been written to specific people known to him, but to the church at large. We call it one of the general or catholic Epistles. The 'twelve tribes' refer not so much to twelve groups of people who were national Israelites by human birth, but to all those who were spiritual Israelites by the second birth; and it is therefore an up-to-date word for all Christians today. If you are a Christian, it is a word for *you*!—because if you are a Christian you are one of the members of what the Apostle Peter calls 'a chosen generation, a royal priesthood, an holy nation' (1 Peter 2:9). You are one of those upon whom God has set His saving love in the Person of the Lord Jesus Christ. You are one of those whose place the Lord Jesus actually took upon the cross when He laid down His life for His sheep, and therefore one of those of whom Jesus said 'no man is able to pluck them out of my Father's hand' (John 10:29). You are one of those who is able to face every trial and difficulty, present or future, in the confidence that 'neither death. nor life, nor angels, nor principalities, nor powers, nor things present, nor things to come, nor height nor depth nor any other creature shall be able to separate us from the love of God, which is in Christ Jesus our Lord' (Romans 8:38–39). The preserving hand of God!

Now just a closing word about James's opening word!—which is simply 'greeting'. There is more to this little word than meets the eye. It does not just mean 'Hello!' The Amplified Bible says that its literal meaning is 'Rejoice!'—and that is certainly the way in which the same Greek word is translated many times in the New Testament. In the matchless Sermon on the Mount, Jesus says 'Blessed are ye, when men shall revile you, and persecute you, and shall say all manner of evil against you falsely, for my sake. *Rejoice*, and be exceeding glad, for great is your reward in heaven . . .' (Matthew 5:11–12). That is it! Whatever the circumstances, the Christian can rejoice, and face the future with confidence, not in the arrogance of his faith, but in the assurance of God's faithfulness.

Chapter 2

TRIALS AND TEMPTATIONS

'My brethren, count it all joy when ye fall into divers temptations; knowing this, that the trying of your faith worketh patience. But let patience have her perfect work, that ye may be perfect and entire, wanting nothing.' (James 1:2–4)

These three verses are among the best known in the whole Epistle, but they nevertheless deserve close and careful study. To help us to do this, let us divide the passage into three sections.

1. *A relationship we ought to foster.* James calls his readers 'My brethren'.

James immediately establishes a relationship with his readers, but let us be careful to note that it is not a relationship enjoyed on any natural basis. People who talk glibly about 'the Fatherhood of God and the Brotherhood of man' often completely misunderstand what the Bible says on this question. There *is* a verse that includes the words 'all the children of God' but we need to notice carefully what it says. Writing to the Galatians, the Apostle Paul says, 'For ye are all the children of God by faith in Christ Jesus' (Galatians 3:26). Nobody can rightly claim to be a member of God's family in a spiritual sense unless they have a personal faith in the Lord Jesus Christ. A man may have knowledge, sincerity, respectability and reputation; he may be a churchman and a communicant; he may have been baptised as an infant or an adult and received into church membership; but unless he has come to put his trust in Christ as his own personal Saviour, he is not a member of the family of God. When the highly religious Pharisees—renowned for their church-going. Bible-reading and prayer-saying—told Jesus 'We have one Father, even God (John 8:4), part of His reply was 'Ye are of your father the devil'! (John 8:44). Here is the clear-cut division between Christian and non-Christian, and the gap is bridged not by ceremony, or ritual, or works of any kind, but 'as many as received Him (the Lord Jesus) to them He gave power to become the sons of God, even to them that believe on His Name' (John 1:12). Are you a member of God's family? Are you *sure*? If not, then look in faith to the Lord Jesus Christ, trust Him as Saviour, and enter now into that wonderful relationship that exists among all the people of God.

Having established this relationship with the Christians to whom he is writing, James does not leave it there! He does not just say to his scattered and persecuted readers, 'I know we are brothers and sisters in Christ, but I am afraid that your difficulties are no concern of mine.' As far as he is able, he enters right into their situation. By writing this letter, he seeks to be a means of blessing and encouragement to them, to bind them together in their 'common salvation' (Jude 3) and to foster that very wonderful relationship. We hear a great deal today about church unity and the ecumenical movement, but one of the greatest mistakes on this issue, and one that is being made by many people, is to think that church unity can be brought about by committees and conferences, discussions and debates, reports and resolutions. That is not what the Bible says! The word 'unity' only occurs twice in the Authorized Version of the New Testament, both times in Ephesians 4. Let us just glance at those two verses, which seem to me to say two important things.

(1) *Church unity is Divine in its conception.* Ephesians 4:3 speaks about 'the unity of the Spirit', or, as The Amplified Bible puts it 'the harmony and oneness . . . produced by the Spirit'. It is the Spirit's work!—something He alone has brought about. Anybody who feels that they must do something to produce one true Christian church is forgetting two fundamental truths: firstly that there already *is* one true church, and secondly that the forming of that church is a Divine work and not one that could ever be accomplished by even the most exalted of churchmen!

(2) *Church unity is doctrinal in its construction.* Ephesians 4:13 speaks of 'the unity of the faith'. While I admit that in context this speaks of a developing unity, the development is linked to the thought of growing in grace and knowledge, and it still remains true that Christian unity is built with the fabric of 'the faith', or what Jude calls 'the faith which was once delivered unto the saints' (Jude 3). It is doctrinal in its construction. It is not the unity of ideas, philosophies, or opinions, nor even a unity of aims as to what the church ought to be doing. It is a unity that has to do with theology rather than action. It is the unity of the faith' as a body of doctrine. It is based on 'things most surely believed' (Luke 1:1) and not on bright ideas enthusiastically held! It is reported that in a Cabinet meeting many years ago, a notable politician once said 'It doesn't matter what we agree on, as long as we all agree'. Whatever the context might have been then, it is a doctrine of devils in the matter of church unity. Yet it is the plausible kind of line taken by so many people. There are those who seem to think that every religious group which has any pro-

fessed link with Christian things, whether it is Roman Catholic, Protestant, evangelical, liberal, modernistic or reformed, can happily be joined together into one impressive universal church invested with great spiritual power and authority. That is the devil's lie! Unity without truth is a building without a foundation, and as such it is bound to collapse. We cannot create church unity; that has already been done by the Holy Spirit. What we *are* to do, by prayer, and concern, and the sharing of burdens, and the practical outworking of the love of God which is 'poured into our hearts through the Holy Spirit' (Romans 5:5, RSV), is to foster and develop the wonderful relationship we already have with all those who love the Lord Jesus in sincerity and truth.

The next point in our passage is this—

2. *A reality we ought to face*—'When ye fall into divers temptations'.

Notice how realistic James is here—he says 'when' and not 'if'! Temptation and testing for the Christian are not matters of 'if' but of 'when'. It may be that the word translated 'temptations' would be better translated 'trials'. Of course there is a difference between the two, and I think it can be put like this: temptations are sent by Satan in order to make the Christians stumble; trials are sent by God in order to make the Christian stand. The author and object are completely different. In testing you, God is aiming at your maturity; in tempting you, Satan is aiming at your misery. Writing on the subject of 'Temptation' in *The New Bible Dictionary*, Dr. J. I. Packer puts it like this—'Satan tests God's people by manipulating circumstances, within the limits that God allows him (cf. Job 1:12, 2:6; 1 Cor. 10:13), in an attempt to make them desert God's will'. We shall need to take a longer look at this, but at this point let us just notice the phrase 'fall into'. It is the Greek word '*peripipto*', and the important thing about it in the context of our present study is that it is the same word as that used about the traveller in the story of the Good Samaritan. In Luke 10:30 we read that he '*fell among* thieves'. Here was an attack not only savage and serious—but sudden! There was no warning, no time to run away, to avoid the issue. The man was going about his normal daily business, when suddenly the attack was on. Now as Christians, we have at least one important advantage over that traveller—and that is that we have been warned of the danger. The Bible says clearly that 'Your adversary the devil prowls around like a roaring lion, seeking some one to devour' (1 Peter 5:8). The same verse tells us that we must therefore 'Be sober, be vigilant', or, as The Amplified Bible puts it, 'Be well-balanced, temperate, sober-minded; be vigilant and cautious at all times'. Speaking in the House of Commons in 1913 on the subject of Naval Defence, the then Mr. Winston Churchill said: 'We must always be ready to meet at our average moment anything that any possible enemy might hurl against us at his selected moment'. This is wonderful advice for the Christian!

This whole subject of temptation is so important, especially to young Christians, that I want us to take a closer look at it, and to hammer out some vital Biblical principles to help us as we face its reality in our lives.

Firstly, temptation will not be removed. We have already noticed that James says, '*when* ye fall into divers temptations . . .', not '*if* . . .'. In a verse we shall look at more closely in a moment, the Apostle Paul reminds the Christians at Corinth that the temptations they faced were 'common to man' (1 Corinthians 10:13), an inevitable and peculiar feature of man's earthly situation. Young Christians especially could well begin any study of temptation by recognizing this simple fact. Becoming a Christian does nothing whatever to remove a person from the sphere of temptation. It is no good looking on earth for a situation that only exists in heaven! Just as Christ's coming into the world did not banish temptation universally, so His coming into the human heart does not banish it personally. Temptation is one of the universal and inevitable facts of life. It is the testimony of the ages that for the Christian temptation is not removed. One of the loveliest descriptions of what God has done in saving the Christian is in Paul's words that He has 'delivered us from the Kingdom of darkness, and transferred us to the Kingdom of His beloved Son' (Colossians 1:13 RSV). In the irresistible and sovereign grace of God we were plucked out of 'the snare of the devil', having been 'taken captive by him at his will' (2 Timothy 2:26), and brought into the family, fellowship and kingdom of God's own people. But mark this! Although we have been taken for ever out of Satan's grip and possession, we have not yet been removed from his interest and attention!

Secondly, temptation is not reduced. Admittedly in the context of trials rather than temptations (though we have seen something of the difficulty in separating the two) the Apostle Paul says 'all that will' (the word means something like 'are determined to') live godly in Christ Jesus shall suffer persecution' (2 Timothy 3:12). That gives us more than a hint of something we can surely see to be true in the matter of temptation, not only in the pages of the Bible, but also in our own experience. Although we are lost to his grip and ownership, and although he is limited by the omnipotent overruling of

God, Satan is relentless in the severity and subtlety of his attacks. It is no mark of maturity to be unconscious of his activities, or to feel that we have reached a stage where we cannot, or ought not to be, sorely tempted. The world's one perfect Man was subject to nothing less than a personal confrontation with the devil for nearly six weeks, as we can read in Matthew 4:1–11, and right through His life we see the signs of temptation, mediated not only through His enemies, but also through His friends. In that fine little book, *The Gospel in Genesis*, Henry Law, a nineteenth century preacher who was at one time Dean of Gloucester, wrote this about Satan's ceaseless ministry of mischief:

> 'He never slumbers, never is weary, never relents, never abandons hope. He deals his blows alike at childhood's weakness, youth's inexperience, manhood's strength and the totterings of age. He watches to ensnare the morning thought. He departs not with the shades of night. By his legions he is everywhere, at all times. He enters the palace, the hut, the fortress, the camp, the fleet. He invests every chamber of every dwelling, every pew of every sanctuary. He is busy with the busy. He hurries about with the active. He sits by each bed of sickness, and whispers into each dying ear. As the spirit quits the tenement of clay, he still draws his bow with unrelenting rage'.

I hope you do not find that depressing—but we must be realistic. I suppose it might be thought wonderful in a way to be able to encourage Christians into believing that the further they went on in the Christian life the less interested in them Satan became, and that eventually they reached a stage when temptation came only very occasionally, and that it then came so obviously and gently that it could be overcome with only the slightest of unaided effort. Perhaps you sometimes feel that that is the way things ought to be! The truth is otherwise! If you study the lives of some of the greatest heroes in Scripture, you will discover that their greatest temptations—and, sadly, their greatest falls—came not at the beginning of their walk with God, but far along the road of discipleship. Moses was the proved leader of God's people, and noted for his meekness, when petulant temper laid him low. David, the man after God's own heart, was already King of Israel when he was shattered by lust. Peter, the man of rock, had already proved his courage many times before he crumbled into cowardice.

Let us be sure that we have grasped the situation so far. Although God has taken us out of the realm of Satan's ownership, He has not removed us from the sphere of his influence; although we may be growing in grace and in our knowledge of Christian things, the severity and subtlety of temptation will remain with us until our dying day, with no promise whatever that it will lessen in its power. Temptation is neither removed at our conversion nor reduced by our consecration. Originally spoken in the context of His second coming, Christ's own word comes with equal urgency and relevance to young and old—'And what I say unto you I say unto all, Watch'! (Mark 13:37).

Not only is it not removed or reduced, but

Thirdly, temptation must be recognized. That is to say, we must understand what temptation is—and we are at least part of the way there when we recognize what it is *not*. If there are four words which could transform the thinking of multitudes of Christians right here, they are these—*temptation is not sin*. What a lot of morbid introspection would be cleared away if this truth were grasped! How many seeds of doubt and defeat have germinated in the soil of ignorance about this point! Yet it is one of the clearest truths in the whole Bible, and one that can be seen by the simplest child and by referring to only one verse of Scripture! In Hebrews 4:15 we read concerning the Lord Jesus Christ—'For we have not an high priest which cannot be touched with the feeling of our infirmities; but was in all points tempted like as we are, yet without sin'. Before I underline exactly how this verse helps us to recognize that temptation is not the same as sin, let me point out something that I have found wonderfully helpful. In describing *our* temptations James calls them 'divers', or as we would say today 'various'. But the phrase used in Hebrews about the temptations, trials, suggestions and persuasions that came to Christ is 'in all points'. In the truest and most terrible sense we can say that all hell was let loose at Him while He was here on earth in the flesh. There was no avenue of temptation, moral, social, physical, material, mental or spiritual along which He was not assaulted. He was tempted to display Himself to the crowds and to despair when He was alone. He was tempted in the hour of shining triumph and in the moment of solitary tiredness. When, after telling us that Jesus was 'in all points tempted' the writer of Hebrews adds 'like as we are', I am sure he is taking in the corporate experience of all Christian people, and then reminding them as individuals that whatever temptation comes to them came first to Him. Let me bring this home to you personally. Are you tempted along the line of pride? So was He. Or selfishness? So was He. Or dishonesty? So was He. Or impurity? So was He. Or compromise? So was He. Or laziness? So was He. You cannot name a single pressure from Satan and circumstances that He did not feel. He was 'in all points tempted like as we are, yet'—and here is the whole glorious point of this verse to our subject—'without sin'. Write that upon your heart!—and determine on the authority of God's Word that you will never again fall for the devil's lie that temptation is sin. How many Christians have slipped into the sin of faithless depression at this point! Yet that depression is not only faithless, but needless and senseless. Jesus was battered by temptation and allurement of every kind, yet emerged from it all without a single stain of sin. Let us learn to recognize the truth of what temptation is—and what it is not!

One last point—

Fourthly, temptation can be repulsed. To put it in another, dramatic way, defeat for the Christian is utterly unnecessary. If there is one verse above all that shows this clearly from the Christian's point of view, it is 1 Corinthians 10:13—'There hath no temptation taken you but such as is common to man: but God is faithful, who will not suffer you to be tempted above that ye are able; but will with the temptation also make a way to escape, that ye may be able to bear it'. In His infinite wisdom, God has allowed us to remain temporarily in a sphere where we are surrounded by temptation, but in His unchanging faithfulness He has not abandoned us there!

Look at the three 'buts' in this great verse, and notice how wonderfully they cement its truths together.

(a) 'There hath no temptation take you *BUT* such as is common to man'. We are for ever trying to excuse our sin by our circumstances. There is the kind of attitude that says 'Of course nobody has my particular problems.' 'If only I didn't live with unconverted parents.' 'The real trouble is the boss at the office.' 'If only I belonged to a keen church.' 'If only my health was better.' 'I am sure nobody has my circumstances. If they did, they wouldn't talk so glibly about overcoming temptation.' Isn't that it? Now this verse makes it quite clear that far from being unique, our pressures and problems are common human experience, shared by multitudes of others. Our circumstances are a normal part of the human situation.

(b) '*BUT* God is faithful, who will not suffer you to be tempted above that ye are able.' However extraordinary it may seem to the untaught Christian, the truth of the matter is that Satan only tempts by Divine permission! The last word in the degree and timing of your temptation is not Satan's but God's. You may sometimes feel that you are no more than a pawn in the hands of a ruthless enemy; but it would be nearer the truth to say that the devil is a pawn in the hands of your heavenly Father. Look again at that phrase—'(God) will not suffer (or "allow") you to be tempted above that you are able'. There is a limit beyond which Satan can never go, and that limit is set by a sovereign and omnipotent God, and exactly suited to your own personal background, temperament and circumstances. Take time to read the first two chapters of the book of Job. You will find them an outstanding endorsement of this bedrock truth.

(c) '*BUT* will with the temptation also make a way to escape that ye may be able to bear it'. The Apostle Peter puts it like this—'The Lord knoweth how to deliver the godly out of temptations' (2 Peter 2:9), and here of course is the clinching point, that the Christian's potential for constant victory is not in His own strength, but in the indwelling grace of the living God, Who is 'able to keep you from falling' (Jude 24).

Summing up verses 2–4 so far, then, we have a relationship we ought to foster—'My brethren'—and a reality we ought to face—'when ye fall into divers temptations'.

These give us the context for the remaining thing that is said here.

3. *Results we ought to find*. 'Count it all joy . . . knowing this, that the trying of faith worketh patience. But let patience have her perfect work, that ye may be perfect and entire, wanting nothing.' Perhaps it will help us if we divide that phrase into three parts, showing us three results we ought to find in our own Christian experience as we meet with the trials and temptations of daily life. Here they are:

(1) We should find that *Gladness is Possessed*. James says 'count it all joy'. He does not say—in the words of a song that used to be popular before teenagers were invented!—'Powder your face with sunshine, put on a great big smile'. The Christian's joy in the heat of testing and temptation is not the result of casual fatalism, but of convinced faith. It is not powder on the outside, but power on the inside! It is not the attitude that says 'I might as well grin and bear it because there is nothing I can do about it', but rather the serene joy of knowing that there *is* something that God can do about it—or, rather, that there is something that He has already done, and something that He is constantly doing. It is significant to notice how often in the New Testament the joy of the early Christians is spoken of in the moments of their severest trials, and therefore of their severest temptations to doubt the goodness and faithfulness of God. Paul says 'with all our affliction, I am overjoyed' (2 Corinthians 7:4, RSV). When Paul and Silas were in prison at Philippi, with their feet fast in the stocks, we read that at midnight they 'prayed, and sang praises unto God' (Acts 16:25). In fact, Paul's astonishing testimony was this—'. . . I take pleasure in infirmities, in reproaches, in necessities, in persecutions, in distresses for Christ's

sake: for when I am weak, then am I strong' (2 Corinthians 12:10). The seeming paradox of the last nine words is the clue to the source of Paul's joy under pressure. It was a joy born of knowing that although he must despair of his own ability to withstand the trials and temptations of life, he could delight in God's promised sufficiency. The Christian's joy under pressure is related to his unconditional confidence in God. How do you personally rank in that important test? There is gladness to be possessed!

(2) We should find that there are *Graces to be Produced*. James goes on—'knowing this, that the trying of your faith worketh patience'. It is a little difficult to separate this second point from the third, because here we already have a hint of the glorious truth that runs through them both, namely that every situation the Christian faces is an instrument in the hand of God for the blessing of the believer! Of course this catches up the first point too. The Christian can rejoice in trials and temptations because these are the means God uses to test his faith and prove its real worth. This is not to say that God tempts the Christian to sin. James especially guards against this misconception in verse 13, to which we shall come later. The word 'trying' here in verse 3 is the word you would use about testing or refining metal. Perhaps a good illustration today would be the testing of aircraft fabric to ensure that it is capable of withstanding the stresses of supersonic flight. What James is saying is that the 'trying', or testing, of faith, 'worketh patience', or, in modern language, produces steadfastness or endurance, and it is in the very nature of the case that these are qualities or graces that can only be produced in the fires of affliction. How can faith be proved without fire? How can ability be shown without

a test? How can a race be won without running? How can a goal be reached without striving? It is a wonderful part of God's overruling economy that the trials and temptations, the pressures and persuasions, the doubts and difficulties in a Christian's life can be taken by Him and used to produce graces and virtues that could not be produced in any other way. As J. M Neale put it many years ago:

The trials that beset you,
The sorrows ye endure,
The manifold temptations
That death alone can cure,—

What are they but His jewels
Of right celestial worth?
What are they but the ladder
Set up to heaven on earth.

That already anticipates our third point. Not only gladness to be possessed and graces to be produced, but

(3) There is *Growth to be Perfected*—'But let patience have her perfect work, that ye may be perfect and entire, wanting nothing'. You see, 'patience' is not the end of the story, it is only part of the means! The end is that we might be 'perfect and entire, wanting nothing'. God's purpose for the Christian is not that he should go through life in a series of spiritual fits and starts, flashing out with the odd bright spot here and there and then sinking back into dullness and defeat, no further ahead. God's purpose and concern for all Christian people, without exception, is that they should grow and develop into a mature and balanced life of holiness, and that every single person brought into the family and fellowship of His people should be 'conformed to the

image of His Son' (Romans 8:29), and to do that, God uses many means. The Bible, of course, and prayer, and Christian fellowship and service. But God uses other means too—and note this very carefully—God uses disciplines, and difficulties, and pain, and temptations, and disappointment, and suffering. It is for the very reason that God is sovereign that He is able to use the devil's lie as well as an angel's lips, the maliciousness of an enemy as well as the ministry of a friend. It is only when we grasp the reality of God's complete control of every detail of the affairs of men that we can begin to apply the truth of Paul's earlier words in Romans 8:28 that 'all things work together for good to them that love God, to them who are the called according to His purpose'. And it is for this reason, and for this reason only, that the Christian can dare, whatever the circumstances, to 'count it all joy'.

Chapter 3

PRAYER'S VITAL SECRETS

'If any of you lack wisdom, let him ask of God, that giveth to all men liberally, and upbraideth not, and it shall be given him.

But let him ask in faith, nothing wavering. For he that wavereth is like a wave of the sea driven with the wind and tossed.

For let not that man think that he shall receive anything of the Lord.

A double minded man is unstable in all his ways.'

(James 1:5–8)

I have called this chapter 'Prayer's Vital Secrets' because basically this is a passage about prayer. It is introduced, however, by a statement which reveals one of man's root problems. We can link all this together if we outline the passage as follows:

Firstly, there are *both sides of a spiritual problem*—On the one side 'If any of you lack wisdom' and on the other side 'God, that giveth to all men liberally, and upbraideth not'.

Secondly, there are *basic secrets of successful prayer*. This section takes in the whole of the rest of the passage, and will therefore form the main part of our study in this chapter.

1. *Both sides of a spiritual problem*. 'If any of you lack wisdom'—'God that giveth to all men liberally' (v. 5).

In a way these two phrases give us a balance-sheet of man's earthly situation, with the liabilities on one side and the assets on the other. Taking the liabilities first, what we see is:

(1) *The deficiency of human reasoning*—'If any of you lack wisdom'. The key to unlock this phrase is, of course, the meaning of the word 'wisdom', and we can begin straight away by saying that it has nothing whatever to do with a person's I.Q. When James talks about 'wisdom', he does not mean intelligence, knowledge, cleverness or education. He is not speaking about mental prowess but about spiritual perception. There is a vast difference between these two. During his education campaign in the nineteenth century, the 7th Earl of Shaftesbury once said 'Education without instruction in religious and moral principles will merely result in a race of clever devils'. In trying to grasp the meaning of what James is saying here we probably need to tune the thing even finer than that and to say that the 'wisdom' of which he speaks means something like the ability to discern God's hand in human circumstances and to apply heavenly judgment to earthly situations. One only has to put it like that to see that we have the right heading for this section—the deficiency of human reasoning! As Elihu said to Job—'Great men are not always wise: neither do the aged understand judgment' (Job 32:8).

We saw earlier on that the unconverted man is incapable of understanding spiritual truth—1 Corinthians 2:14 makes it plain that '. . . the natural man receiveth not the things of the Spirit of God: for they are foolishness unto him: neither can he know them, because they are spiritually discerned'—but we need to remember that the Christian, too, is incapable of making right judgments if he relies merely on his own powers of reasoning. It is part of the Holy Spirit's ministry in the Christian's life to wean him away from trusting in merely mental resources and to look and listen for another, higher wisdom. This has a really practical application. Here is a crisis in your life, or at least a situation where two or more courses are open to you. It may be something that only affects you, or it may affect many others. It may be the question of a life partner, or a change of job, or the issue of full-time service, or a policy decision in the home. Very carefully you weigh up the pros and cons from a rational point of view. The issue seems to lean in one direction. So far so good. But there is one vital, overruling factor that must be brought into the situation before you can safely move, and that is the 'still, small voice' of God. Without this, all human reasoning is deficient. Have you ever noticed the first things for which the Apostle Paul prayed on behalf of the Christians at both Ephesus and Colosse? '. . . making mention of you in my prayers; that the God of our Lord Jesus Christ, the Father of glory, *may give unto you the spirit of wisdom and revelation* . . .' (Ephesians 1:16–17); 'we . . . do not cease to pray for you, and to desire *that ye might be filled with the knowledge of His will in all wisdom and spiritual understanding* . . .' (Colossians 1:9–10). When God gave King Solomon a blank cheque and invited him to 'Ask what I shall give thee', Solomon reminded Him of the circumstances and responsibilities of his life and said 'Give therefore thy servant an understanding heart . . . that I may discern between good and bad' (1 Kings 3:9). Both Solomon and Paul, the greatest men of their days, recognised the deficiency of human reasoning. We should do the same!

Turning now to the assets on the balance-sheet we find

(2) *The sufficiency of Divine resources*—'God, that giveth to all men liberally, and upbraideth not'. The

Amplified Bible has a wonderful note about those first three words. It says that the literal meaning is 'the giving God'. Here is the language of faith! It is characteristic of the unbeliever to see God with a clenched fist; it is characteristic of the believer to see Him with an open hand. The unbeliever sees God as a stern law-giver, cold, hard, difficult to please. The believer, while increasing in his understanding of God's uncompromising holiness, sees Him more and more as a loving Heavenly Father, unfailingly concerned with the blessing of His children.

The story is told of an old woman who lived alone. She was so poor that she found it difficult to pay the rent to keep a roof over her head. One morning, the local Minister called to see her. He knocked at the door several times, but as there was no reply he went away. That afternoon, he called again, and getting no reply at the door he looked in at the window. The old woman sat huddled over a few smouldering embers in the fireplace. When she looked up and saw him, she immediately went to the door and welcomed him in. 'I called this morning', he said, 'but there was no reply'. 'Oh, I heard you knocking', she answered, 'but I thought you had come to collect the rent.' If we make that mistake about God, if we see Him as only concerned with demanding His due, then in the words of the old hymn writer,

> '*. . . we magnify His strictness*
> *With a zeal He will not own*'.

When God gives, He gives 'liberally, and upbraideth not', that is to say, He does not give according to our worthiness, or gratitude, nor does He withhold from us because we ask too much or too often. God's generosity is measured by what He designs and not by what we deserve. And among all the multitude of gifts which He longs to pour out upon us, there is the gift of that 'wisdom that is from above' (James 3:17).

To recognize that is to recognize as never before the need to obey those familiar words in Proverbs 3:5–6:

> 'Trust in the Lord with all your heart, and do not rely on your own insight. In all your ways acknowledge Him, and He will make straight your paths'.

Here, then, are both sides of a spiritual problem—man's basic inability to make spiritual judgments, and God's infinite wisdom which He is always willing to bestow. Before we get into the second part of the passage, it is worth spending just a moment more with the wonderful truth that when God gives He 'upbraideth not', that is to say He does not give in order to get, nor does He keep on reminding us that 'it is our turn to pay'! We sometimes sing a hymn written by Frances Ridley Havergal in which these words are put into the mouth of the Lord Jesus—

> *'My life was given for thee.*
> *What hast thou given for Me?'*

What is not generally known is that later on she changed those words, putting them this time into the mouth of the Christian, and making them read—

> *'Thy life was given for me.*
> *What have I given for Thee?'*

Do you see the difference? It is always right for the Christian to be searching his heart in the light of the cross, and seeking to present himself 'a living sacrifice, holy, acceptable unto God . . .' (Romans 12:1), but it is *not* right to have a picture of Christ standing forlornly outside of a person's selfish and ungrateful life, almost regretting that He had died for them at all, and measuring His gifts according to their gratitude. When God gives, He gives 'liberally, and upbraideth not'.

Yet there *are* conditions to be fulfilled before certain blessings can be experienced, and while James rejoices in the truth of God's generosity, he also reminds us that gifts such as 'wisdom', or spiritual insight, need to be asked for before they can be received. That brings us to the heart of what James wants us to learn from verses 5–8:

2. *Basic secrets of successful prayer.*

> 'let him ask of God . . . but let him ask in faith, nothing wavering. For he that wavereth is like a wave of the sea driven with the wind and tossed. For let not that man think that he shall receive anything of the Lord.
> A double minded man is unstable in all his ways.'
> (vv. 5–8)

I have used the word "successful" deliberately, because that is precisely the kind of prayer of which James is speaking. Look at the end of verse 5—'it shall be given him'. At the beginning of the verse we have a Christian with a need. He has a problem he cannot solve, a crisis he cannot overcome. He is unsure of the way, uncertain of the truth. At the end of the verse the clouds have lifted and everything is clear. The answer, the wisdom, has been 'given him'. What comes in between these two situations is obviously tremendously important, yet it is contained in three words—'let him ask'. This is the first of three basic secrets James gives us in these verses. To make them hang more tidily in our minds, we will use one word for each of them. The first is this:

(1) *Our prayer must be definite.* 'Let him ask' (v. 5).

Somebody once said 'The real secret of prayer is secret prayer', and even if that is over-simplifying things, at least it helps to get rid of a lot of pious humbug. There is probably no other religious subject about which Christians profess so vastly, yet practice so vaguely. It is so easy to talk about prayer, to say how much we believe in it, to say how important it is, but the really important thing is this: do we pray? Surely it must be one of the most pathetic paradoxes in Christendom that while we evangelicals make such capital out of our understanding of the doctrine of justification by faith, and our freedom of access to God in prayer without the mediation of priest or ritual or ceremony or sacrifice, it is almost universally true that our prayer meetings have the poorest attendance of any part of our church programme! If only our concern to pray could match our willingness to serve on committees! If only we could get on our knees to plead with God as readily as we stand on our feet to preach to others! It sometimes seems to me that we have got our thinking on this so far out of focus that in the average church the prayer meeting is an added extra to give impetus to the organization, rather than an expression of the fellowship's corporate conviction that, in Hudson Taylor's fine words, we should 'learn to move man, through God, by prayer alone'.

But the whole truth cuts a little deeper! Isn't the paltry prayer meeting just a reflection of the private devotional life of the church's individual members? And isn't their devotional life a thermometer of their spiritual health? Somebody has said 'What a man is on his knees before God, alone, that he is and no other'. *Read that through again!—Slowly!* By that definition, do you need to make a radical re-assessment of your spiritual standing? Are you so caught up with your activities, your programme, your preaching, your organizations, that you are making the miserable mistake of confusing activity with progress?

When the Lord sent Ananias to minister to the newly-converted Saul of Tarsus, the one mark of recognition he gave him was 'behold, he is praying' (Acts 9:11 RSV). Is that the distinguishing mark of your life?—or are you just a good preacher, a good Sunday School teacher, a good worker, a good organizer? There is a world of difference between having the ability to organize and inform others and having the kind of prayer life that would make true of you what Andrew Bonar once wrote about Robert Murray McCheyne—'He dwelt at the mercy-seat as if it were his home'. That tribute may remind you of the opening words of Psalms 91—'He that dwelleth in the secret place of the most High shall abide under the shadow of the Almighty'. An old Arabic translation of the last part of the verse puts it like this—'(he) shall always be in touch with the Almightiness of God'. In the context of our constant need, what more incentive could we ever have to be men and women who 'Pray without ceasing' (1 Thessalonians 5:17).

'If any of you lack . . . let him ask'! In the context of our need—James has been speaking about a person lacking wisdom, or spiritual insight, in facing up to life's problems and responsibilities—God's word of command is clear: we must pray. This is underlined in James 4:2 where the Apostle says quite bluntly '. . . ye have not, because ye ask not'. It is no good wringing our hands when we ought to be bending our knees! 'If any of you lack . . . let him ask'! For too many of us, the well-known words of Joseph Scriven are too well known:

O what peace we often forfeit,
O what needless pain we bear—
All because we do not carry
Everything to God in prayer.

A theoretical knowledge about the mechanics of prayer is no substitute for the practice of praying. Just to clinch this question of the need to be definite in our prayer, look again at these three words—'let him ask'. Surely they suggest at least two irresistible incentives.

Firstly, *the way is open.* '*Let* him ask . . .' If it is not too casual a phrase, we can say that God's blessing is there for the asking! At the very moment when Jesus died on the cross we read that back inside the city of Jerusalem '. . . the curtain of the temple was torn in two, from top to bottom' (Matthew 27: 51 RSV). Here was a dramatic visual aid used by God to show that the Old Covenant was at an end, and the barrier to God removed. The door shut by man's sin had been opened by Christ's sacrifice. When He died He bought the right for every Christian to have instant, constant access to the heart of God, and to His throne of grace. If only all Christians could grasp this truth, and apply it to their own lives! The devil cannot prevent God answering our prayers, but he does all he can to prevent us asking, and he often does so by twisting the truth that we are not worthy to ask. Now that *is* true! If we were only able to pray effectively when we were worthy, or when we deserved to be heard, or when we could bring to God a standard of obedience and holiness that gave us the right to be answered, then we would never be able to pray at all. And is it not true that again and again what prevents us from praying is precisely that feeling of unworthiness? 'What is the use of praying?—I feel such a hypocrite.' 'I feel so far away from God.' 'I have lost my faith.' 'I can't possibly pray while I am backsliding like this.' 'I have got to the stage where I don't want to pray.' Have you ever felt like that? Do you feel like it now? Then listen again—'. . . the curtain of the temple was torn in two from top to bottom'. Your access to God is assured not by your attitude but by an act of God! However weak, helpless, depressed, sinful, weary or heavy laden you are, however out of touch you feel, however far you have backslidden, however long it has been since you last prayed, you *can* come, *now*, into the presence of your Heavenly Father. You need no ceremony, no elaborate preparation, no ecclesiastical ritual, no costly sacrifice, no human mediator. The way is open —'Let us therefore come boldly unto the throne of grace, that we may obtain mercy, and find grace to help in time of need' (Hebrews 4:16).

Secondly, *the worth is obvious*. 'Let him *ask* . . .' Many centuries ago, St. Chrysostom wrote:

> 'The potency of prayer has subdued the strength of fire, it has bridled the rage of lions, hushed anarchy to rest, extinguished wars, appeased the elements, expelled demons, burst the chains of death, expanded the fates of heaven, assuaged diseases, dispelled frauds, rescued cities from destruction, stayed the sun in its course, and arrested the progress of the thunderbolt. There is an all-sufficient panoply, a treasure undiminished, a mine which is never exhausted, a sky unobscured by clouds, a heaven unruffled by the storm. It is the root, the fountain, the mother of a thousand blessings!'.

Its worth is obvious!

It is impossible to read the Bible, the biographies of Christian heroes, or even the experience of our own lives without realizing the obvious worth of prayer. In facing the pressures and problems of daily living, prayer substitutes our weakness by God's strength, our ignorance by His wisdom, our emptiness by His fulness, our poverty by His wealth, our doubt by His certainty, our impotence by His omnipotence. Its worth is obvious! Isaiah's words still hold good today—'He giveth power to the faint; and to them that have no might he increaseth strength. Even the youths shall faint and be weary, and the young men shall utterly fall: But they that wait upon the Lord shall renew their strength; they shall mount up with wings as eagles; they shall run and not be weary; and they shall walk, and not faint' (Isaiah 40: 29–31).

How perfectly that all fits into the context of what James is saying! 'If any of you lack . . . let him ask . . .'! How perfectly it meets our need day by day! And how perfectly it suits the character of 'The giving God'! Prayer is not wrestling with God's reluctance to bless us, but rather laying hold upon His willingness to prove Himself true to His own nature and Word. Prayer is a means of grace, and the grace of God, but its very definition, is full, and free, and sufficient for all men. God's constant desire is the highest good of each one of His children. There is not a single Christian for whom God does not long to 'open you the windows of heaven, and pour you out a blessing, that there shall not be room enough to receive it' (Malachi 3:10). So let our prayer be definite!

Over a hundred years ago, Jane Crewdson wrote a hymn which sums this all up so perfectly, that it is worth quoting freely:

O fount of grace that runneth o'er,
So full, so vast, so free!
Are none too worthless, none too poor,
To come and take of Thee?

We come, O Lord, with empty hand;
Yet turn us not away;
For grace hath nothing to demand,
And suppliants nought to pay.

'Tis ours to ask and to receive:
To take and not to buy;
'Tis Thine in sovereign grace to give,
Yea, give abundantly.

And thus, in simple faith, we dare
Our empty urn to bring;
O nerve the feeble hand of prayer
To dip it in the spring!

Now to the second secret of successful prayer:

(2) *Our prayer must be dogmatic*—'But let him ask in faith' (verse 6).

Have you ever noticed, in reading the New Testament, what a tremendous premium is placed on faith? The writer of Hebrews goes so far as to say that 'without faith it is impossible to please Him (God)' (Hebrews 11:6), and if in that chapter it refers especially to the initial act of faith when a person comes to put their trust in God as Saviour, we certainly cannot restrict faith's importance to that context. The characteristic mark of a Christian's developing relationship with God is that it is a walk of faith—in 2 Corinthians 5:7 Paul says '. . . we walk by faith, not by sight'. Moreover, faith is something which God commands. Of course this is true in terms of the initial act of faith. When the crowds asked 'What must we do, to be doing the works of God?'

Jesus replied 'This is the work of God, that you believe in Him whom He has sent' (John 6:28–29 RSV). But it is also a command for the Christian in his daily life. In that classic passage in Ephesians, where Paul speaks of the Christian life in terms of spiritual warfare—and how closely that ties up with this opening chapter of James's Epistle!—he says that we are to 'stand therefore . . . above all, taking the shield of faith, with which you can quench all the flaming darts of the evil one' (Ephesians 6:14 and 16 RSV).

When we come specifically to the subject of prayer, the New Testament is no less insistent on the importance of faith. Jesus says 'And whatever you ask in prayer, ye will receive, if you have faith' (Matthew 21:22 RSV); and again, 'Whatever you ask in prayer, *believe* that you receive it, and you will.' (Mark 11:24 RSV) Writing to a man responsible for guiding others in spiritual things, the Apostle Paul says 'I will therefore that men pray everywhere, lifting up holy hands, *without wrath and doubting*' (1 Timothy 2:8).

Now if faith is a command, then the absence of faith is disobedience of the revealed will of God, and disobedience, in the very order of things, is something which God cannot possibly bless. So James does not just say 'let him ask'; he adds 'but let him ask in faith'.

Three important points need to be made here in order to give a clear grasp of what James means.

The first point is this: Verse 6 begins with a 'But'! 'Let him ask', says James in verse 5, 'But let him ask in faith'. Prayer is not merely presenting God with a spiritual shopping-list. Nowhere are we promised answers to prayers on the sole condition that we trot out a sequence of words addressed to God, any more than the formula "through Jesus Christ our Lord' is a guarantee that our prayer will be effective. James makes it very clear that we are not to be like those who 'think that they shall be heard for their much speaking' (Matthew 6:7). If prayer is to be effective it must be what James later calls 'the prayer of faith' (James 5:15).

The second point is this: Notice very carefully that James says 'Let him ask *in* faith', not 'let him ask *with* faith'. Faith is not an additive which gives our prayer more impetus. It is the essential attitude of heart of the person who prays. Faith is not something that is added to a man's prayer; prayer is something that issues from a man's faith, from the conviction of a man's heart. The Bible puts it like this—'For whoever would draw near to God must believe that He exists and that He rewards those who seek Him' (Hebrews 11:6 RSV). Do you have a clear grasp of that? Not only is it pointless to go through the motions of prayer without faith, but it is equally futile to think that we can ask for anything we like, provided we can somehow or another screw ourselves up to add faith to the petitions! We cannot just add faith to prayer in the way that we stick a 'Personal Delivery' stamp on an envelope containing an important letter. We are to ask *in* faith, not just *with* faith. The model prayer, given by Jesus in Matthew 6:9–13, begins, if you look carefully, with a statement of faith, followed by petitions based on its truth—

'Our Father which art in heaven'—there is the statement of faith.
'Hallowed be Thy name. Thy Kingdom come. Thy will be done . . .'—there are the petitions.

The third point is this: It is sometimes easy to think of faith as being a kind of spiritual shot in the dark, or at least a step into the unknown. But that is not strictly true, or at least it is not the whole truth. I remember hearing a friend of mine once say 'I am called to worship a God I cannot see, but not to submit to a God I cannot know and prove'. Do you see how this applies to our present context of prayer? When we speak of praying in faith, we do not mean having faith in prayer! Nor do we mean faith in a proposition. We mean faith in a Person, in the living God, in One who cannot fail, cannot lie and cannot deny Himself. Our faith is not in the hope that we can pray well enough, nor in the hope that the theoretical 'laws' of prayer will work if we do. It is faith in the God of the Bible who says 'I am the Lord, I change not' (Malachi 3:6). This takes us to the very heart of things, that in fact our faith is not to be thought of in terms of the absence of knowledge, but in the application of the knowledge we have! In Robert Keen's fine words—

'How firm a foundation, ye saints of the Lord,
Is laid for your faith in His excellent Word'.

The greater our knowledge of God, the more certain our faith will be. To put it more intimately, the more we know of God's likes and dislikes the more will our prayers be according to His will—and it is the prayer that is according to His will that God promises to answer. In one of his writings, E. Stanley Jones tells how this came across to him—'In prayer I seldom ask for things, more and more I ask for God Himself, for the assurance that His will and mine are not at cross-purposes, that we are agreed on all major and minor matters. I know then, if this is so, I'll get all the things I need'.

'Let him ask in faith', says James. But not blind faith. Faith is invisible, but not irrational. It is faith in God. To pray in faith is to pray confidently in the knowledge of God's nature and in the growing knowledge of His will.

Our prayer must be definite. Our prayer must be dogmatic. So to the final thing these verses have to say—

(3) *Our prayer must be decisive*—'. . . nothing wavering. For he that wavereth is like a wave of the sea, driven with the wind and tossed. For let not that man think that he shall receive anything of the Lord. A double minded man is unstable in all his ways' (vv. 6–8).

In a sense, this third point is an elaboration of the second, but it is worth looking at separately if only because James himself elaborates it with the illustration of verse 6. Three words will help us to see this section more clearly:

Firstly, *there is a searching condition*—'nothing wavering', or, as The Amplified Bible puts it, 'with no wavering—no hesitating, no doubting'. In his commentary on the Epistle of James, Dr. C. Leslie Mitton says 'These words underline what is meant by the prayer of faith. The thought that his request may not be answered simply does not enter the mind of the one who prays. Misgiving has no place at all, and in consequence his attitude is totally free from hesitation'.

Secondly, *there is a simple comparison*—'For he that wavereth is like a wave of the sea driven with the wind and tossed'. Let me illustrate the illustration! I live at present in the town of Weston-super-Mare. Situated on the north-west coast of Somerset, Weston-super-Mare faces the Atlantic, and more often than not there is a bracing wind blowing in from the West. Weston-super-Mare is also at the mouth of the River Severn, giving a considerable flow of water from the North. In addition, there is a very fast tide-race which, on the ebb-tide, flows out from the East. The result of all this movement and pressure is that the water in the bay is often very choppy, disturbed, unsettled,—'driven with the wind and tossed'—and, as I know to my cost, a small-boat trip in those conditions can be very uncomfortable! Uncomfortable, too, is the position of the person who prays without real faith and conviction, whose mind is filled with conflict and confusion. What are the winds that can blow a man off course when he comes to pray? There are at least three:

(a) *The wind of unsound doctrine.* In Ephesians 4:14 Paul says that God's purpose and provision for His people is 'that we henceforth be no more children, tossed to and fro, and carried about with every wind of doctrine, by the sleight of men, and cunning craftiness, whereby they lie in wait to deceive'. This emphasizes what we have already seen, that the prayer of faith is based on man's knowledge of God, and of His nature and will. There is a direct link between our knowledge of the Word of God and intelligent prayer. Faith is not ignorance saying 'Believe it and it will be true'; it is intelligence saying 'It is true, believe it'.

(b) *The wind of unusual difficulty.* Acts 27 records part of the Apostle Paul's journey to Rome. In spite of his advice, the ship sailed from Fair Havens, bound for Phenice, but soon ran into the treacherous hurricane Euroclydon. After three desperate days, and when the ship itself was in danger of breaking up, one of the eye-witnesses reported 'all hope that we should be saved was then taken away' (Acts 27:10). It was at that stage that Paul stood in the midst of the passengers and crew and told how he had heard from an angel that, although the ship would be lost, every man aboard would be saved—'wherefore, sirs, be of good cheer, for *I believe God* that it shall be even as it was told me' (Acts 27:25).

Paul's faith was not the result of whistling in the dark. It was the outcome of his personal relationship with God and of the word of God which he had received. Do we allow unusual difficulties to shake our confidence in God? Do we have anything more than a fair-weather faith?

(c) *The wind of unyielded desire.* The heart of this point really belongs to verses 7 and 8, to which we shall come in a moment, but it is certainly not out of place to mention it here. If the prayer of faith, the prayer asked in accordance with the will of God, is one that God will *always* answer, then these verses make it plain that the prayer of the 'double minded man' is one He will *never* answer! This 'wind' is the inward pressure of the old nature, that makes our mind a spiritual storm-centre. We find ourselves not praying for things we desperately need, and going through the motions of praying for things we dare not want. Augustine gave the world a perfect example of this when he confessed that his prayer was once 'Lord make me pure, but not yet'. To put it bluntly, James tells us that that kind of prayer is useless. Our prayer must be single-minded. In the Church of England services of Morning Prayer and Evening Prayer, the Minister, in exhorting the people to make what is called the General Confession, says 'Wherefore I pray and beseech you, as many as are here present, to accompany me with a pure heart, and humble voice, unto the throne of the heavenly grace . . .' Before I was converted, I can remember being puzzled about those words 'with a pure heart'. If one had a pure heart, there was surely no confession to make! And if one did not have a pure heart, one was not, apparently, qualified to make a confession. The explanation, of course, as I later discovered, is that 'pure' means whole-hearted, sincere, or, as James would say 'nothing wavering'. God does not need perfection before He will hear and answer our prayers, but He must have whole-heartedness.

A searching condition—'nothing wavering'; a simple comparison—'For he that wavereth is like a wave of the sea driven with the wind and tossed'. One more thing—

Thirdly, *there is a sad consequence*—'For let not that man think that he shall receive anything of the Lord. A double minded man is unstable in all his ways'. The Revised Standard Version puts this very helpfully—'that person must not suppose that a double-minded man, unstable in all his ways, will receive anything of the Lord'. It has rightly been said that grace is free but not cheap. In the same way, we could say that while prayer is not answered as reward for merit, answers cannot be obtained without meeting the very clear conditions laid down in the Word of God. These two verses are probably among the most severe that James writes. They tell us of a man with a barren prayer life, a man who is going through the motions without receiving any of the benefits, a man who never seems to be getting through to God. Have you ever known what it is to make a whole series of telephone calls through the operator, and to have every call met with 'I'm sorry, but there's no reply'? When a man's prayer life is like that, it is time for him to search his heart to see whether he is asking in the right way. Do you need a re-assessment at this point? Are you praying in faith? Without wavering? With a single eye to the glory of God?

O Thou by Whom we come to God,
The Life, the Truth, the Way,
The path of prayer Thyself hast trod;
Lord, teach us how to pray!

Chapter 4

LIFT UP YOUR HEARTS!

'Let the brother of low degree rejoice in that he is exalted:

But the rich, in that he is made low: because as the flower of the grass he shall pass away.

For the sun is no sooner risen with a burning heat, but it withereth the grass, and the flower thereof falleth, and the grace of the fashion of it perisheth: so also shall the rich man fade away in his ways.

Blessed is the man that endureth temptation: for when he is tried, he shall receive the crown of life, which the Lord hath promised to them that love Him.

(James 1:9–12)

In his spiritual classic *A Serious Call to a Devout and Holy Life*, William Law once wrote 'How ignorant, therefore, are they of the nature of religion, the nature of man and the nature of God, who think a life of devotion to God to be a dull uncomfortable state, when it is so plain and certain that there is neither comfort nor joy to be found in anything else!'

We have already come across this vein of truth in our opening studies in the Epistle of James. His very first word to the persecuted and oppressed people to whom he originally wrote was 'Greeting!'—literally, 'Rejoice!' (verse 1). In verse 2 he tells them that even when they find themselves surrounded by trials and temptations, pressures and problems, they are to 'count it all joy'.

The point he is daring to make is that joy is meant to be the normal experience of every Christian in every circumstance, because of their unconditional confidence in the overruling power and goodness of God.

Coming now to verses 9–12 we see James returning to this theme. Verse 9 shows that even Christians with little or nothing of this world's goods should 'rejoice', verses 10–11 show the reasons why Christians at the opposite end of the social scale can be glad, and verse 12 gives a reason why all Christians can look forward with joyful hope. The whole section, then, is permeated with joy, and in getting its message across, James takes general issues and focuses them in individual terms. These three people, he says, can lift up their hearts.

1. *The man in poverty.* 'Let the brother of low degree rejoice in that he is exalted' (v. 9).

The word 'brother' tells us straight away that James is referring to a Christian, and the description 'of low degree' simply means 'poor' or, as The Amplified Bible puts it, 'in humble circumstances'. It is to this person, to the man with little or nothing in the way of earthly possessions, that James says 'Rejoice!' In materialistic, worldly terms, this makes nonsense, of course. For most people, the feeling is that happiness goes hand in hand with prosperity, while misery and poverty are almost inevitably linked in their minds. But James is not speaking in material terms, but spiritual, and it is in this sense that he is able to say that the poor man who becomes a Christian is automatically, and as the result of his becoming a Christian, 'exalted', regardless of whether there is then or later any change for the better in his material circumstances. In what way, then, is a man exalted when he becomes a Christian? Here are some which I have chosen because of their special application to a person of limited material and financial means.

Firstly, he has a new wisdom. It has often been true—though more in the past than now—that poverty and ignorance have gone together, or that limited means have meant limited opportunities for education. Certainly many of the very poor Christians of the 1st Century would have lacked the special tuition and knowledge of their richer contemporaries. But knowledge and wisdom are not the same thing! Back in 1860, a philosopher called Jeremy Bentham said 'If we can get universal and compulsory education by the end of the century, all our social and political and moral problems will be solved'. How wrong he was! Man needs something higher than knowledge before his own life, let alone the society in which he lives, can be properly managed and conducted. He needs the 'Wisdom' or spiritual insight, of which James has already spoken in verse 5. And that wisdom is not a matter of education, but revelation; not something man learns, but something God gives. The Apostle Paul says that God 'is the Source of your life in Christ Jesus, whom God made our wisdom, our righteousness and sanctification and redemption' (1 Corinthians 1 : 30 RSV).

This is not to despise education, of course. A Christian has a duty to equip himself thoroughly for his life's work. But even if he finds himself at the lower end of the social scale, and without the benefits of higher education, he can rejoice that God has given him the tremendous advantage of spiritual insight, 'even the hidden wisdom, which God ordained before the world unto our glory' (1 Corinthians 2 : 7).

Secondly, he has a new wealth. I am always fascinated by the stories of poor people, or at least people in very ordinary circumstances, who suddenly receive a letter from a solicitor telling them that some long-lost relative has died, leaving them a vast fortune. One day, they are among those 'of low degree', and the next day they are millionaires, not because of a life-time of effort, or as the result of industrious ingenuity, but simply because they have entered into the benefits of somebody else's death and have thus become heirs to a fortune. In some cases, it is literally a case of rags to riches. Now that is the Christian's position! Jeremiah writes of the unconverted 'Surely these are poor; they are foolish: for they know not the way of the Lord, nor the judgment of their God' (Jeremiah 5.4), but the Apostle Paul reminds all Christian people that '. . . we are the children of God: And if children, then heirs; heirs of God, and joint-heirs with Christ . . .' (Romans 8:16–17).

Rags to riches again!—and all as the result, not of our own effort, but of the death of Christ and the grace of God. Somebody cleverly used an acrostic to describe 'grace' as meaning Great Riches At Christ's Expense, and that agrees precisely with what Paul says in 2 Corinthians 8:9—'For ye know the grace of our Lord Jesus Christ, that, though he was rich, yet for your sakes He became poor, that ye through His poverty might be rich'. The Christian is a spiritual millionaire. 'In everything ye are enriched by Him' (1 Corinthians 1:5). Do we live according to our means?

Thirdly, he has a new wardrobe. I remember once noticing that a friend of mine, though having a limited income, always seemed to be very well-dressed. I could never understand how she managed it, until one day she told me 'I have a friend abroad who is extremely wealthy, and she keeps on sending me clothing she buys and then does not bother to wear'! Now the unconverted man's wardrobe is pretty pathetic! Isaiah goes so far as to say that 'all our righteousnesses are as filthy rags' (Isaiah 64:6). Even the best moral and religious efforts of the unsaved are no better in God's sight than dirty rags. The Christian, on the other hand, has a new wardrobe. For instance, God has given him the robe of justification, which means that he can look forward with confidence to the day when he will be able

> *'Clothed in His righteousness alone*
> *Faultless to stand before Thy throne'*.

But God has also given him a complete outfit for daily living on the way! In other words, God has given the Christian the potential for living a holy life, something which he never had before his conversion. You will find some of the resources listed, in this kind of language, in Paul's letter to the Colossians—

> 'Put on then, as God's chosen ones, holy and beloved, compassion, kindness, lowliness, meekness, and patience, forbearing one another and, if one has a complaint against another, forgiving each other; as the Lord has forgiven you, so you must also forgive. And above all these put on love, which binds everything together in perfect harmony' Colossians 3:12–13 RSV).

The Christian—however poor materially—has a new wardrobe, the potential for pleasing God in his daily life. No wonder James says he should rejoice! But notice carefully that what God has provided, we must 'put on'. Our sacred privilege is matched by a searching responsibility.

To sum up, 'the brother of low degree' can rejoice because he has a new wisdom (the gift of spiritual insight denied to the unconverted, however intelligent they might be), a new wealth (unlimited spiritual resources at his disposal as an heir of God), and a new wardrobe (the moral potential of pleasing God).

2. *The Man with plenty.*

'But the rich, in that he is made low: because as the flower of the grass he shall pass away.

For the sun is no sooner risen with a burning heat, but it withereth the grass, and the flower thereof falleth, and the grace of the fashion of it perisheth: so shall the rich man fade away in his ways.'

(vv. 10–11)

Here is a man in quite different circumstances—in plenty, not poverty—and he also can rejoice, not primarily at his material success, but at his new spiritual standing. Rather than attempting a close exposition of the words, let me try to show their general meaning. James's picture is of a comparatively well-to-do man who has been converted, and his point is that just as the poor Christian has special grounds for rejoicing, so has the wealthy man. Here are two of the things we can note about him:

Firstly, he has a new position—'he is made low' (verse 10). That would certainly be a new position for a wealthy man in a society where money could buy favour and popularity very easily. To be rich was to be popular. But prosperity and popularity are treacherous twins, and the human heart being what it is, a man enjoying a great deal of both of them could soon find, like Uzziah, that 'his heart was lifted up to his destruction' (2 Chronicles 26:16). Now converted, the rich man finds himself in an entirely new position. His business colleagues would probably reject him, his friends would avoid him as a religious crank. For the first time in his life he would find that his money had lost its voice. A new position! But as a Christian in grace and knowledge, he learns to rejoice in this new position. He does not, of course, seek to be unpopular and offensive, but he recognizes that there is a reason for his basic rejection by the world, a reason given in Christ's own words when He said 'If you were of the world, the world would love its own; but because you are not of the world, but I chose you out of the world, therefore the world hates you' (John 15:19 RSV).

Secondly, he has a new perspective.

'. . . because as the flower of the grass he shall pass away.

For the sun is no sooner risen with a burning heat, but it withereth the grass, and the flower thereof falleth, and the grace of the fashion of it perisheth: so also shall the rich man fade away in his ways.' (vv. 10–11)

James shows this new perspective by way of illustration. Up until now, the rich man had looked at everything in materialistic terms. His whole outlook on life had been geared to things he could weigh, see, feel, touch, count or take to the bank! Now, says James, he can see how futile that kind of attitude is. Without spending time squeezing detailed meanings out of individual words, look at the general drift of the illustration. The green grass, promising so much in beauty and colour, is soon scorched and withered by the searing heat of the Middle East sun. Notice the sad sequence—'withereth' . . . 'falleth' . . . 'perisheth'. The point is obvious—'so also shall the rich man fade away in his ways.' Paul says the same sort of thing—'the form of this world is passing away' (1 Corinthians 7:31 RSV). The man who puts his trust in earthly values and material possessions is a fool, because he is trusting the temporary.

I have never actually worked it out mathematically, but I am told that the central verse in the Bible is Psalm 118:8. If that is so, then it is a very telling coincidence for the verse reads 'It is better to trust in the Lord than to put confidence in man'! Here is a new perspective, one which every Christian ought to have. No man has life properly in focus until he sees it in the context of eternity. This applies to problems as well as possessions—'While we look not at the things which are seen, but at the things which are not seen; for the things which are seen are temporal; but the things which are not seen are eternal' (2 Corinthians 4:18). So the man in poverty can rejoice, and so can the man with plenty. James now goes on to mention someone else—

3. *The man under pressure.*

'Blessed is the man that endureth temptation: for when he is tried, he shall receive the crown of life, which the Lord hath promised to them that love him.'

Although this verse could well be taken as the beginning of the next section (which would then be vv. 12–16) it can equally be seen to follow on exactly from the verses we have just been studying. Like the grass of the field, man's life is not the end of his prospects, but the fulfilment of them! Think again of the man with what some would call life's advantages, the wealthy man, perhaps a businessman. All of his life he would have been concerned about stocks and shares, deals and agreements, speculations and prospects. All of them would inevitably entail a certain amount of risk, and even if everything went right, temporary prosperity was all he could gain. Now see the difference when he is converted! Admittedly he has to face problems and pressures

('Temptation' in verse 12 is better translated 'trial'), but he is increasingly discovering God's enabling to endure them. And what about his prospects?—'The crown of life'; the eternal honour of living in God's presence. The element of risk?—Nil; 'he shall receive'. The guarantee?—'The Lord hath promised.' Is it any wonder that James encourages the Christian to rejoice? He has a new prospect, one that is based not on his own ingenuity or effort, nor one that runs the risk of falling through because of fluctuation in the stock market, nor one that will prove temporary or unsatisfactory when it finally materializes—but one that the Apostle Peter describes as 'an inheritance incorruptible, and undefiled, and that fadeth not away, reserved in heaven for you, who are kept by the power of God through faith unto salvation ready to be revealed in the last time' (1 Peter 1:45). And what is true of the wealthy Christian under pressure is obviously true of the Christian who is not so well-off financially.

The story is told of two old friends who lay dying. One was a rich but unconverted man, the other a poor Christian. Talking to a visitor about his friend, the unconverted man said 'When I die, I shall leave my riches. When he dies he will go to his!' Here is the radical difference between Christian and non-Christian, believer and unbeliever. Here, above all, is the reason for our rejoicing! Fanny Crosby has put it into words that millions have made their triumphant testimony:

Great things He hath taught us, great things He hath done,
And great our rejoicing through Jesus the Son;
But purer, and higher, and greater will be
Our wonder, our transport when Jesus we see!

Lift up your hearts!

Chapter 5

SIN FROM START TO FINISH

'Let no man say when he is tempted, I am tempted of God: for God cannot be tempted with evil, neither tempteth He any man:

But every man is tempted, when he is drawn away of his lust and enticed.

Then when lust hath conceived, it bringeth forth sin: and sin, when it is finished, it bringeth forth death.

Do not err, my beloved brethren!'

(James 1: 13–16)

I sometimes feel that in terms of Biblical knowledge the average Christian's most urgent need is not to learn a vast amount of new doctrine, but to get a firmer grip on the basic teaching he has already heard. It is interesting to note that when the Apostle Peter was writing his Second Epistle he said 'I think it right, as long as I am in this body, to arouse you by way of reminder' (2 Peter 1: 13 RSV). If we are slow to grasp new truth, we are not slow in forgetting, or in forgetting to apply, the truth we know. The Apostle James seems to have known something of this human failing, because in these verses he returns to a theme he has already mentioned, namely the question of trials and temptations.

It will help us if we divide the passage into four sections.

1. *There is a definite reality.* '. . . when he is tempted' (v. 13).

We saw in verse 2 that when James refers to temptations in a Christian's life, he uses 'when' and not 'if'. We also noted that in that verse it is difficult to decide whether James is referring to temptations (incitement to commit sin) or trials (tests and difficulties)—though in either case 'when' is the right word to use. In verse 13, however, he obviously means the first of these, as the rest of the passage shows. These words help to underline another principle we discovered when dealing with the subject of temptation, namely that the Christian is subject to sharper and subtler temptations than the unbeliever. When a person becomes a friend of God he becomes the enemy of Satan, and can expect to be attacked at any time, at any level, and along any avenue. The Christian who thinks otherwise, and who imagines that he will gradually outgrow temptation as he matures in the faith, has already fallen for one of the devil's cleverest lies. As Samuel Rutherford once put it—'The greatest temptation out of hell is to live without temptation'. Temptation, even for the Christian, is a definite reality.

2. *There is defective reasoning.* 'Let no man say . . . I am tempted of God: for God cannot be tempted with evil, neither tempteth He any man' (v. 13).

The words 'God cannot be tempted with evil' open up such a wonderful line of truth in themselves that I want us to leave them over to the end of this chapter and to a section on their own. Our second point, then, is this: Let no man blame God when he finds temptation too strong for him. God tempts nobody.

It seems that James wrote this passage to counteract defective reasoning which ran something like this: 'God created all things. Therefore God must have created the evil impulse in man, and in that sense must be said to have created sin. So God is responsible for the sin in my life.' Well, that kind of argument rings a bell! Man is a past master of the art of evading his personal responsibility. Somebody once said that in the Garden of Eden 'Adam blamed Eve, Eve blamed the serpent, and the serpent didn't have a leg to stand on!' But what a serious truth we have here! What an indication it is of the depravity of the human heart, and of the depth of inbred sin, that in a moment of crisis, when things go seriously wrong, when a man has a bad moral fall, or makes a fatal mistake, he can not only seek to avoid all personal blame, he can actually flash his fist in God's face and say that He is responsible.

Nobody seems to be sure whether verse 16 belongs to this passage (vv. 13–15) or the next (vv. 17–18)—but I feel certain that it would be just at this point that James would want to say 'Do not err, my beloved brethren'. Do not make the mistake of blaming God for your failure, and backsliding, and sin. Write this in letters six feet high!—*God may call you to endure difficulties, but He will never cause you to experience defeat.*

That leads us on to see the next thing these verses teach—

3. *There is a decisive responsibility.*—'But every man is tempted, when he is drawn away of his own lust, and enticed. Then when lust hath conceived, it bringeth forth sin: and sin, when it is finished, it bringeth forth death.' (vv. 14–15)

This is a graphic description, in James's favourite picture-language, of the origin and result of sin. The illustration he uses is one of birth. He says that sin, as it were, has two parents, one inward and one outward. It will help us if we trace the sequence in four stages, with a single word to identify each one:

(a) *Condition.* 'His own lust' does not necessarily mean a person's perverted or exaggerated sexual urge, but it does mean a man's inbred desire to do wrong. No understanding of sin holds together without a grasp of this truth, that every man has within him that fallen, perverted nature that is constantly capable of the worst crime in the most terrible evil. Jesus made it plain that sin of every kind, be it word, thought or deed, 'come from within, and defile the man' (Mark 7:23).

(b) *Consideration.* '. . . drawn away of his own lust and enticed'. Man not only has the potential for sin, he is surrounded by the possibilities and prospects. James uses the word 'enticed', which means something like 'taken with a bait'. It is a fisherman's word. I remember once walking along the seashore at St. Ives, in Cornwall, and seeing a man pull in one fish after another. When I asked what bait he was using, he said that all he had was a silver spinner on the hook. The fish were attracted by the glitter, swam towards it, opened their mouths, and were on dry land before they could change their minds! If your experience of fishing is like mine, you never seem to come across fish like that!—but if you have the average experience of life, you will recognize the parallel situation very readily. Inwardly, we have the desire and the potential to sin. Outwardly, there is the enticement, the allurement, the temptation. So far, we are safe. Temptation, as we saw in an earlier study, is not sin. But this consideration, this toying with the idea, this allowing of the thing to occupy a place in our minds, moves us towards the fateful moment.

(c) *Conception.* 'Then when lust hath conceived, it bringeth forth sin'. The natural desire, faced with the opportunity and enticement, is now joined by the will, which puts the desire into action, and it is this assent of the will to what the outward enticement has offered to the inward desire that fertilizes temptation and turns it into sin. This is the moment of decisive responsibility. As somebody put it—'It takes two to make a successful temptation, and you are one of the two'. Take time to study some of the Bible's classic examples of the way in which sin can be seen in the process of conception, for instance: Genesis 3:1–6; Genesis 38:12–18; 2 Kings 5:20–21. And then remember that these things 'were written for our learning'! (Romans 15:4).

(d) *Conclusion*. 'And sin, when it is finished, bringeth forth death'. Here is the certain, tragic result of sin. 'The wages of sin is death' (Romans 6:23) is the Bible's unwavering verdict. That is not only a terrible warning to the unconverted to turn to Christ before it is too late; surely it is also a solemn measure of the Christian's responsibility to 'preach the Gospel to every creature' (Mark 16:15) and a motive to 'put on the whole armour of God, that ye may be able to stand against the wiles of the devil' (Ephesians 6:11).

A definite reality; defective reasoning; decisive responsibility. We can now go back to consider the six words I deliberately left out of our detailed study a few moments ago. They tell us that

4. *There is a divine reliability.*—'. . . God cannot be tempted with evil' (v. 13).

This, to me, is one of the most exhilarating phrases in the Bible. Let me show you why! I sometimes feel that as Christians we spend far too much time looking inwards to our own failures and outwards to our circumstances, and not nearly long enough looking upwards to see the nature and character of our God, and saying with the hymnwriter 'How Great Thou Art!' Surely it does not need a particularly vivid imagination to see some of the God-glorifying truths that flow from this one simple statement that 'God cannot be tempted with evil.' It is like a scintillating diamond, every facet of it sparkling with spiritual brilliance.

Firstly, His Person can never be defiled. I remember once speaking at a Town Hall in the South of England. On the way in to the meeting, I saw a young man in the foyer. I had never seen him before, and even then only glanced at him in passing, but I remember thinking 'that man is unclean'. This may sound terribly unkind, but let me finish the story. A couple of hours later, when the meeting was over and I was leaving the Hall, a steward told me that a man wanted to speak to me. To my surprise, it was the man I had noticed on the way in. We found a quiet room, and I asked him why he wanted to talk to me. In a few moments he had reached the heart of his problem—a girl, a friendship, immorality that had now got out of control. Why I should have been given such a sense of the truth before I ever met him, I do not know, but I do know this, that in the translated words of the French proverb, 'Sin makes ugly.' It scars and stains. It leaves its mark on the soul and sometimes on the body. It dulls the mind, dims the eye, loosens the grip. In the words of Jesus, it 'defiles the man' (Mark 7:23).

But the Lord our God can never be defiled, because He cannot be tempted with evil. Do we ever think deeply and gratefully enough about this? It is one thing to grow in our knowledge of God's power, and in our sense of His wisdom, but do we grow in our appreciation of His perfect holiness? How often do we adore Him for being 'altogether lovely'? (Song of Solomon 5:16). To get there is to get to a place of real worship.

Secondly, His purposes can never be deflected. I sometimes think that the devil loves us to make promises to God!—or at least I feel that he is never very worried by them! He knows perfectly well that the high and holy resolution, made in the heat of the moment, can so easily be deflected into compromise and the second best, and even into miserable defeat. Peter's 'I will not deny you' (Mark 14:31 RSV) never caused the devil a moment's worry! The sharp-eyed maid was already coming on duty, and the fire was being lit in Caiphas's courtyard. There would be ways to deflect Peter!

But God's purposes can never be deflected, because He cannot be tempted with evil. When, at the beginning of Psalm 115 we have the implication that things seem to be going badly for God's people so that the heathen cry 'Where is their God?' (v. 2 RSV) the Psalmist's triumphant reply is 'Our God is in the heavens; He does whatever He pleases' (v. 3 RSV). God's word to His people was 'I work, and who can hinder it?' (Isaiah 43:13 RSV). The eternal purposes of God can never be deflected. He is slowly but surely working them out to His own glory. Although 'God moves in a mysterious way' it is nevertheless 'His wonders to perform'!

Thirdly, His perception can never be dulled. Ours can! How often have you made the wrong decision, adopted a wrong attitude, missed a vital opportunity, because your perception has been dulled by sin, not least by the sin of being out of touch with the Lord. I know that I have and, unless I miss my guess, you know the experience so well that there is no need to elaborate the point here. Instead, let us revel in this truth, that because God can never be tempted and touched by sin there is never a moment of day or night, in shadow or sunshine, when He does not know, understand and appreciate our precise circumstances and our exact need. The Psalmist says 'He determines the number of the stars. He gives to all of them their names. Great is our Lord, and abundant in power; His understanding is beyond measure' (Psalm 147:4–6 RSV). Get a grip of that! Infinite understanding of the minutest detail of your life! Not just cold, analytical, critical knowledge, but warm, loving, compassionate understanding that is always moving to meet you at the point of your personal need!

Fourthly, His power can never be diminished. How directly and devastatingly sin robs a man of power! And how faithfully the Bible records it! Lot chooses the plain and people of Sodom (Genesis 13:10–13) and in no time he is just a pathetic, powerless has-been. (Gen. 19:14). Samson breaks his vow, and the tiger becomes a toy (Judges 16:25). The disciples of Jesus, given authority to 'cast out devils' (Mark 3:14–15) find themselves reduced to impotence (Mark 9:18). When they asked Jesus why they had failed, the answer was clear (Mark 9:29)—disobedience. The men of wonders had been reduced to men of words.

But the sin that saps the Christian's strength can never affect the power of God. He cannot be tempted with evil; the ravages of sin cannot affect Him, because they cannot touch Him. God never weakens. He is never 'off colour' or 'one degree under'; never less than omnipotent. And that almightiness is available at every moment for every Christian! Writing to the Ephesians, Paul says that he has been praying that they might know '. . . the immeasurable greatness of His power in us who believe, according to the working of His great might which He accomplished in Christ when He raised Him from the dead and made Him sit at His right hand in the heavenly places'. (Ephesians 1:19–20 RSV). Notice that! The same power that raised Christ from the tomb is at work to raise you to a life that is pleasing to God. The *same* power! Undiminished! His touch has still it's ancient power!

Fifthly, His promises can never be devalued. 'Devaluation' is a word we can all understand in days of economic crisis. Our banknotes still have the words 'I promise to pay the bearer on demand . . .' but the promise hardly seems to hold good! More seriously, how often have our own promises, to God or to man, been devalued by faithless rationalism, by clever compromise, or by some other means.

How vastly different are the ways of God! The Bible teems with the promises of God from Genesis to Revelation, and not one of them has He ever failed to keep to the full! At the dedication of the temple in Jerusalem, Solomon's opening words to the congregation were 'Blessed be the Lord that hath given rest unto His people Israel, according to all that He promised: there hath not failed one word of all His good promise, which He promised by the hand of Moses his servant' (1 Kings 8:56). Christians all down the ages have been able to echo Paul's words about Christ 'He carries out and fulfils all God's promises, no matter how many of them there are; and we have told everyone how faithful He is, giving glory to His name' (2 Corinthians 1:20, The Living New Testament).

As we take a careful look at our lives, at the way in which we were brought to Christ, at the provision of our every need, at moments of guidance, at all the multitude of events and circumstances that have brought us to this point in time, surely we can never dispute the fact that we have a promise-honouring God!

What is more, the Bible is overflowing with untapped streams of blessing for the days ahead. There are promises on every page, ours to claim and enjoy. Many, of course, have conditions attached, conditions which we must fulfil But if we do, we will find God true to His nature and His word, keeping His promises to the hilt—'God cannot be tempted with evil'!

Chapter 6

GIFTS AND THE GIVER

'Every good gift and every perfect gift is from above, and cometh down from the Father of lights, with whom is no variableness, neither shadow of turning.'

(James 1:17)

Here is a verse that is wonderfully simple—and simply wonderful! It seems to me to deal with three related subjects, and so that we can hold it clearly in our minds right at the beginning, here is the outline:

First of all we have *Human giving*—'Every good gift'; then we have *Heaven's gifts*—'every perfect gift is from above'; finally we have *The Heavenly Giver*—'and cometh down from the Father of lights, with whom is no variableness, neither shadow of turning'.

Let us look in detail at each of the three in turn.

1. *Human giving.*—'Every perfect gift'.

There is one rendering of these three words that appeals to me very much, and it is this: 'All giving is good.' Now I know that that is an obscure rendering and that you will not find it generally supported, but I still have more than a feeling that this may well be what James had in mind. You see, the Greek word for 'gift' is a different word to the one used later on in the verse, in the phrase 'every perfect gift'. The word in this opening phrase usually means the act of giving, and if our line of approach is right here, what James is saying is that there is a general element of good in all acts of giving. A gift does not have to have a religious or spiritual context in order to have something good about it. A good gift can be made by a thoroughly bad man. Jesus made that clear in Matthew 7:11 when He said '. . . ye then, being evil, know how to give good gifts unto your children . . .' Let us never be cynical about generosity. There is a general element of good in all acts of giving.

Nevertheless, there is one important qualification we need to make just here, and that is that all our human giving, however well meaning, generous or sacrificial, is always marred in some way by our very humanity. Here are some of the ways in which our giving is spoilt.

(a) *It may not be sincere.* There is such a thing as giving in order to get! It is not only in fishing that people can use a sprat to catch a mackerel! There is the kind of giving that is crafty, clever, calculated. You can read a terrible example of this in the story of Simon the sorcerer, recorded in Acts 8. There is the kind of giving that looks like generosity, but in fact it is ingenuity. Let us beware of that, and let us give out of a sincere heart, with a pure motive.

(b) *It may not be sensible.* I remember once staying in a Pastor's home over the weekend, and on Sunday morning, as I looked out of my bedroom window, I saw the next-door neighbour loading his golf clubs into his car and then driving off down the road, waving to his little son as he left. Later, I asked the Pastor what this man was like. He replied 'He is very well off, yet the home is not happy. He just lives for the golf course. He gives his wife and son every kind of gadget or toy they ask for, but he deprives them of himself as a husband and father'. Now we cannot condemn him for the gifts he made;

there was an element of goodness in them. But it was not wise giving. It was not sensible.

(c) *It may not be sufficient*. That is obvious, surely. We hear of a need, an appeal for help, and after thinking about it we send off our 50p Postal Order, or £5 cheque, or whatever it is. Fine! There is an element of good in that, perhaps even a great deal of good. The gift might even be generous to the point of sacrifice, but if the appeal is the kind I seem to receive almost every day, the gift will probably not be sufficient to meet the need at the other end. Now remember that the simple point I am trying to expose here is that our human giving has limits to it, and it is limited not least in this, that it is not always sufficient to meet the need to which it is given. Good, but not sufficient.

(d) *It may not be suitable*. I am sure you will not find it difficult to fill in an illustration here! The presentation cigarette case given to the man who doesn't smoke! . . . the bowl of perfumed shaving soap to the man who uses an electric shaver! . . . the sixth set of fruit spoons received as a wedding present! Good gifts, all of them, and marked, perhaps, with genuine generosity, but spoilt because not suitable.

Summing up then, there are two things we can say about human giving: because it is human *giving*, there is an element of good about it—'all giving is good'—but because it is human giving it is marred, limited in some way. It may not be sincere, it may not be sensible, it may not be sufficient, it may not be suitable. One thing is certain—it is limited by our humanity.

That leads us straight on to the second thing James deals with in this verse:

2. *Heaven's gifts*—'every perfect gift is from above'.

Writing in 1 Corinthians 15:49 about the contrast between the believer's life on earth and in heaven, the Apostle Paul uses the phrases 'the image of the earthy' and 'the image of the heavenly', and it seems to me that we could well apply those phrases to the subjects of giving and gifts. Our human giving and gifts bear 'the image of the earthy'; they are limited by their earthliness in one way or another. But God's giving and gifts bear 'the image of the heavenly'. In complete contrast to ours, they are always sincere, always sensible, always sufficient and always suitable. They are not mixed with earthly alloy. As the Bible puts it 'The blessing of the Lord makes rich, and He adds no sorrow with it' (Proverbs 10:22 RSV). Let this simple truth he riveted in your mind: *nothing good comes except from God, and nothing except good comes from God!* In a word, His gifts and giving are perfect—and that is exactly the word James uses. In fact, James uses the word several times in his Epistle, each time with its own subtle shade of meaning. In 1:4 it means 'mature'; in 1:25 it means 'faultless'; in 3:2 it means 'fully developed'. Here is the word that sums it up—'perfect'! Let us just stay with that word for a little while, because it is one of the Bible's favourite words in describing the mind and activity of God. Here are just some instances of its use that spring immediately to mind:

(a) *His work is perfect*. 'He is the Rock. His work is perfect'. (Deuteronomy 32:4). Here is one of the great distinguishing lines between something man does and something God does. You look at something that man has done, and on the surface it looks good. It looks wonderful. You might almost say it looks perfect. Then you begin to examine it a little more closely and when you do so you begin to discover the flaws and failures that are in one sense an exposition of the whole of human nature. The closer you examine something that has the mark of man upon it, the more imperfect you see it to be. On the other hand, the closer you examine something that has the mark of God upon it, the more do you see it to be perfect. As a single illustration, take a needle, produced by the most modern manufacturing process. To the naked eye, it is perfection itself, smooth-surfaced and with its point almost invisible, but put it under a microscope and its smooth surface is now pitted and pock-marked, and its point no more than a jagged stump. On the other hand, think of a common flower. As you walk along a country path, you stop to admire a bank of wild flowers and say 'My, those flowers are perfect!' But stop for a moment longer, pick one of them, take it into a laboratory and place it under a microscope. Now take a closer look! The perfection you saw in passing is as nothing compared with the perfection you now see. A miniature world of design and delicacy revealed in all its amazing intricacy. The deeper and closer you examine any work of God, the more wonderfully and fully do you see it to be perfect.

Now what are the two greatest works of God? Surely these—the work of creation and the work of redemption. Or, if you prefer, the work of creation and the work of re-creation. As far as the work of creation is concerned, what is the recurring refrain of the first chapter of Genesis? Here it is—'God saw . . . that it was good' (v. 4); 'God saw that it was good' (v. 10); 'God saw that it was good' (v. 12); 'God saw that it was good' (v. 18); 'God saw that it was good' (v. 21); 'God saw that it was good' (v. 25); and finally, as if to underline and emphasize and bring it all to a head 'And God saw everything that He had made, and, behold, it was very good'. God's work of creation was perfect!

And what of God's work of redemption, of re-creation? There is an amazing phrase in Isaiah 53:11 which says that 'He shall see of the travail of His soul, and shall be satisfied'. Have you ever meditated upon that staggering sentence? Here is God saying that as far as the whole question of man's redemption is concerned, at the end of the day He will be satisfied—satisfied with all that He has done, with all that the work of redemption has achieved. Now this says something most important about all the questions that men raise on this issue: But what about heathen who have never heard the Gospel? And what about Christians who fail in their responsibility to witness? And what about children who die before reaching the years of discretion? And what about those who have gone through the whole of life mentally incapable? They are vast questions; so vast that I cannot pretend to be able to begin to answer them in detail; but I do know this—that the Lord will be satisfied. The work of redemption is in God's eyes complete, and a completely satisfying work. Take that to your heart, even if you cannot grasp it in your head! 'His work is perfect'!

(b) *His way is perfect*. 'As for God, His way is perfect'. (Psalm 18:30). David wrote those words after his deliverance from the hand of Saul. It had been a period of great testing and trial, darkness and difficulty, misunderstanding and misery. David had gone through very deep waters. There had been things that in the flesh he would have gladly avoided. Had he been able to choose out his own way, he would surely have chosen not to go the way of Saul's wrath and anger and militancy against him. He would have gone another way. But now he looks back on it all and says 'As for God, His way is perfect'. He says, as it were, 'I can see now.

I have gone through the valley of the shadow; through the fire; through the deep waters; through the testing; and I can see now that God's way is perfect, and that all these things have been parts of God's maturing work in my life'.

There are times when every Christian finds a 'Why?' in his mind. Circumstances have suddenly turned sour, problems have multiplied, resources have vanished, faith has turned to fear, and clarity to cloud. In times like these, how wonderful it is to be able to recognize that the Eternal God is ordering *all* our ways, and that 'His way is perfect'! Paulus Gerhardt's words, translated by John Wesley, turn our hearts in exactly the right direction:

Leave to His sovereign sway
To choose and to command;
So shalt thou wondering own His way,
How wise, how strong His hand.

Far, far above thy thought
His counsel shall appear,
When fully He the work hath wrought
That caused thy needless fear.

(c) *His will is perfect*. The obvious verse here is Romans 12:2 where Paul speaks about knowing 'what is that good and acceptable and perfect will of God'—or, in the words of the alternative reading given in The Amplified New Testament, 'even the thing which is good and acceptable and perfect in His sight for you'. Notice that! God's will is not just perfect in a vast, general, universal sense, but in a personal, individual sense too. It is perfect 'for you'!

(4) *His word is perfect*. In just a few verses' time, James is to describe God's word as 'the perfect law of

liberty (v. 25), and Psalm 19:7 says that 'The law of the Lord is perfect, converting the soul'. Here is just one reason why the Bible is never out of date, never out of touch, never out of context. It is always perfect.

Gathering all these up, God's work is perfect, His way is perfect, His will is perfect, His word is perfect—and so, too, says James, are His gifts. They are perfect,—perfectly suited both to His design and to our development.

All giving is good; even gifts from sinners to sinners have an element of good about them. But the only perfect gifts are those which come from God, and, like every facet of God's nature, and every outworking of His purposes, they are perfect in every way.

Now to the final point in these verses—

3. *The Heavenly giver.*—'and cometh down from the Father of lights, with whom is no variableness, neither shadow of turning.'

In this phrase, we have something said about God's Name, and something about His Nature. Let us look at these in turn.

Firstly, God's name—'the Father of lights'. I am sure that you have sometimes stood at night on a hill, or other raised ground, and looked across a dark valley lit by a million different points of light coming from homes and factories, street lamps, advertising signs, and many other places. I remember once doing this on Castle Hill looking out over Huddersfield and the surrounding towns, and thinking as I did so that all these lights probably came from one basic source. In a moment, my mind was here in James 1:17, turning over James's unusual—I almost added 'illuminating'!—little phrase 'the Father of lights'. What a rich vein of truth there is locked up in those few words. Think of some of the 'lights' of which God is the Father, the Author, the Source.

(a) *Natural light.* God's first spoken word recorded in the Bible is 'Let there be light' (Genesis 1:3). God is the creator of the sun, the moon and the stars. 'The heavens are telling the glory of God; and the firmament proclaims His handiwork' (Psalm 19:1 RSV).

(b) *Intellectual light.* Daniel 2 includes the story of Nebuchadnezzar's troubled dreams. None of the wise men of Babylon could interpret the king's strange vision, and they were sentenced to death. Daniel, next in line for execution, held a prayer meeting with his companions, Hananiah, Mishael and Azariah, and in answer to their prayers, God revealed the secret of the King's dream to Daniel. The story goes on, 'Then Daniel blessed the God of heaven. Daniel said: 'Blessed be the name of God for ever and ever, to whom belong wisdom and might. He changes times and seasons; He removes kings and sets up kings; He gives wisdom to the wise and knowledge to those who have understanding. He reveals deep and mysterious things; He knows what is in the darkness, and the light dwells with Him' (Daniel 2:19–22 RSV). There is never any conflict between true science and the Bible. Every true discovery is simply God's gift of intellectual light.

(c) *Theological light.* By this, I do not just mean the truth that is put in the well-known words of Psalm 119:105—'Thy word is a lamp unto my feet and a light unto my path'. What I mean is that the light of God's word cannot be seen and understood and appreciated and applied unless God Himself explains it and opens it up to us. The perfect illustration of this is in the story of Philip and the Ethiopian eunuch in Acts 8. When Philip drew up to the chariot, the eunuch was reading from Isaiah 53, but it seems that he was not getting on very well, because when Philip asked him if he understood what he was reading he replied 'How can I, except some man should guide me?' (Acts 8:31). He needed the Spirit-filled Philip to explain God's Word to Him and without that help he found the Scriptures dark and meaningless. In exactly the same way we need the enabling of the Holy Spirit to explain the Bible's meaning today. Let us never forget this! Every time we come to the Bible, whether we have been a Christian for a few weeks, or months, or for many years, our right attitude must be this: 'How can I understand, unless Someone should guide me, and unless that Person is the Holy Spirit?'

God is the Father of theological light, the essential Revealer of truth about Himself. That is why the Apostle Paul says in 1 Corinthians 2:14 '. . . the natural man receiveth not the things of the Spirit of God: for they are foolishness unto him: neither can he know them, because they are spiritually discerned'. Unless God the Holy Spirit makes the Gospel clear and relevant to an unconverted person, then all the programme and the preaching and the praying and the preparation that might be brought to bear upon that person will not result in his conversion. It *must* be the work of the Holy Spirit, breaking in with light into that person's mind, and showing him the truth of the Word of God relative not only to himself but also to the Lord Jesus Christ as the only Saviour from sin. Even when a person becomes a Christian, he is no less dependent upon the Holy Spirit to reveal Divine truth from the printed page. As William Cowper puts it:

The Spirit breathes upon the Word
And brings the truth to sight;

Precepts and promises afford
A sanctifying light.

(d) *Spiritual light.* This is different from theological light, or perhaps more accurately is part of its practical outworking. In 1 Peter 2:9, Christians are told to 'show forth the praises of Him who hath called you out of the darkness into His marvellous light' and the Apostle Paul says 'For once you were darkness, but now you are light in the Lord; walk as children of light' (Ephesians 5:8 RSV). The state of being born again, a child of God, a Christian, is described in the Bible as being in light in contrast to darkness, and of that light, the light of eternal life, God is the sole and sovereign Author.

Of all these lights, then, natural, intellectual, theological, and spiritual, God is the Father, the Author, the Source. How right the Apostle John is when he says that 'God is light, and in Him is no darkness at all' (1 John 1:5).

Secondly, God's nature—'with Whom is no variableness, neither shadow of turning'. There is a principle and a picture here, and a look at each of these will close our study of this verse.

(a) *The Principle.* Believe it or not, the most exciting word for me in this phrase is the word 'is'! The only way I can explain its meaning here is to say that the phrase 'is no' literally means 'can be no'. Do you see the difference? James is not merely saying that with God there has been no variableness so far, nor just that God is not variable at the moment, *but that with God variableness is impossible*, that a changeable, variable God is a contradiction in terms. He is not saying that God has not changed so far, but that God can never change. God says with wonderful clarity 'I am the Lord, I change not' (Malachi 3:6) and we are told of the Lord Jesus that He is 'the same yesterday and today, and for ever' (Hebrews 13:8). That is the principle. Now notice—

(b) *The Picture*. '. . . no variableness, neither shadow of turning'. This is a very difficult phrase, on which commentators have spilled a great deal of ink. Yet perhaps in general there is an uncomplicated answer. After all, this is a picture, one taken from the sky, the natural heavens. The sun gives light, but not always to the same degree, because it is not always at the same angle. There is dawn, high noon, twilight, dusk. The sun's light varies and changes. James in fact adds one more detail and speaks of a 'shadow of turning', that is to say a shadow caused by turning in the eclipse of the sun. Now in trying to grasp the exact details of what James is saying in this verse we could thread our way through margins and manuscripts until we were all hopelessly confused. Instead, let us turn again to The Amplified Bible which, as so often, puts it in the clearest way—'in the shining of Whom there *can be* (notice that!) no variation (rising or setting) or shadow cast by His turning (as in an eclipse)'.

Let me underline one word as we close this chapter—the word 'His'. Life may have its shadows—it almost certainly has—but they are never caused by *His* turning, by *His* changing! They may be caused by ours, because we have changed our position. If you stand exactly under a street lamp, no shadow is cast. Take one step away from the light and you find a shadow in front of you. Not a very big one, but a shadow nevertheless, and one caused by your turning, or changing your position. Take a few more steps, and the shadow grows; more steps, and it grows bigger yet. Go far enough away and you will be in total darkness. Now that is the picture. There is never a shadow in your life because God has turned. If there are shadows, it may be because you have changed your position. You have gone away. You have moved a step, or more than one, from being right under the light of His revealed will. If so, be sure of this: the further away you go, the darker and deeper the shadow will be! Turn back! Turn back now! And as you do so, remember that with God there is no turning, never a shadow in your life because He has turned, proved unfaithful, broken His Word. T. O. Chisholm puts it to poetry—

'Great is Thy faithfulness', O God my Father,
There is no shadow of turning with Thee;
Thou changest not, Thy compassions they fail not.
As Thou hast been Thou for ever wilt be!

Great is Thy faithfulness! Great is Thy faithfulness!
Morning by morning new mercies I see.
All I have needed Thy hand hath provided;
Great is Thy faithfulness Lord unto me!

Chapter 7

SO GREAT SALVATION

'Of His own will begat He us with the word of truth, that we should be a kind of firstfruits of His creatures.' (James 1:18)

In the last chapter we were concerned, in our study of James 1:17 with gifts and giving, and with the name and nature of the God who, as James had said earlier, 'giveth to all men liberally' (1:5). Coming now to verse 18, we see that James writes about the greatest gift of all, the gift of the new birth, which places a person into the family of God.

The whole verse hinges around the three words 'begat He us', or as The Amplified Bible puts it, 'He gave us birth'. As the Apostle Peter puts it in praising God—'By His great mercy we have been born anew to a lively hope through the resurrection of Jesus Christ from the dead' (1 Peter 1:3 RSV).

In some Bibles, Ephesians 2 is headed 'What we were by nature and what we are by grace', and the chapter is full of vivid contrasts between the state of believers and unbelievers. The whole chapter is a development of two little phrases—'at that time' (v. 12) and 'but now' (v. 13). Just look at some of the contrasts:

v. 12	'without Christ'	v. 13	'In Christ Jesus'
v. 12	'aliens'	v. 19	'fellow citizens with the saints'

v. 12	'strangers'	v. 19	'the household of God'
v. 13	'far off'	v. 13	'made nigh'
v. 15	'enmity'	v. 15	'peace'

There is a wonderful Bible study for you!—some of the ways in which Christ has transformed the state of the believer. Yet the most vivid contrast of all is not one of the five we have just noticed. This comes earlier in the chapter. Look at the opening words of the chapter —'And you he made alive, when you were *dead* through the trespassses and sins in which you once walked . . .' (RSV). The same staggering contrast is put like this a little further on—'But God, who is rich in mercy, out of the great love with which He loved us, even when we were dead through our trespasses, made us alive together with Christ . . .' (vv. 4–5 RSV). Here is the greatest contrast of all! Once, we were dead, slain by sin. Now we have been given life. We have not just been improved, or morally strengthened, or given a new vision or outlook. It is not that a sort of inherent godliness has been fanned into a flame. What has happened is a miracle that has transformed deadness into life. Anything less than that is less than a real appreciation of what the Lord has done in bringing us unto Himself. I dare not pass this point without asking you this simple, personal question—have you been born again? If not, then you do not belong to the Kingdom of God. You may be religious, you may be sincere, you may be a churchgoer, you may be generous, you may be serving the church, you may be a preacher, you may be a Sunday School teacher, a Bible Class leader, but unless you have been born again then you are not a member of God's family. This is the inescapable and only starting place of the Christian life. Jesus said 'Except a man be born again, he cannot see the Kingdom of God' (John 3:3). No amount of respectability, sincerity or religion can take the place of God's miracle of re-birth.

Now come back to James 1:18. If you look closely, you will notice that it draws our attention to three things about the new birth: firstly, its infinity—'of His own will'; secondly, its instrument—'with the word of truth'; and thirdly, its intention—'that we should be a kind of firstfruits of His creatures'. Let us look at each of these in turn.

1. *The infinity of new birth*—'of His own will'. The new birth is an infinite thing. I mean by that that it is not something merely of earth, time and space, but of heaven, eternity and infinity. To try to get this into focus, let me put it in three ways.

Firstly, it is infinite in its being. The story is told of a visiting speaker at a school who was asked 'What was God doing before He created heaven?' The speaker thought for a moment and then said 'I am not sure, but I think He must have been creating hell for people like you who ask questions like that!' I must say that I have never been asked that particular question—though I have used the story to help in dealing with others!—but I have often been asked 'Why did God create man?' I wonder what your answer would be? It seems to me that the Bible gives only one specific answer to that question, and that is in Revelation 4:11 where we read 'Thou hast created all things, and for Thy pleasure they are and were created'. The words 'for Thy pleasure' could literally be translated 'by Thy will', so that we find these two thoughts inseparably intertwined. We can turn the issue around in our minds as much as we like, but eventually we come back to this point, that all the Bible tells us as to why God created man is this: it was for His pleasure, it was by His will. It pleased Him to do so.

If that is why God created man, why does He recreate men? What is the reason behind a man's re-birth? Here is the Bible's answer, in James's words—'of His own will begat He us'. The Bible takes us no further. The only Biblical reason given for a man's salvation is that God willed it. That is why I am using the word 'infinite' here. Infinite in its being. The whole conception and idea and plan of man's new birth must be seen in its ultimate context—it was of God's own will. A man's new birth is not limited or decided by anything or anyone else. I would think that nearly all Christians would come at least part of the way here. They would agree that their salvation is not the result of their own merit, or works, or effort. But there are many Christians who would add 'I know that I did not *earn* my salvation, but without getting too involved in deep and dark theology doesn't the Bible say something about foreknowledge? And doesn't that mean that God saw in advance those who of their own free will would choose to repent and believe, and then having seen that these people would take the initiative of repenting and believing, He decreed that these people would be saved?' Now there are many people who think along those lines—and I must confess that there was a time when I not only thought like that but I believed it and preached it. Yet surely this is unsatisfactory for one very simple reason—it places the Creator in the hands of the creature. God's purposes are suspended until the creature decides that something will be done. Now surely anything that does that is not only unsatisfactory but unsound, unscriptural. It makes the grace of God dependent upon something else, and once grace becomes dependent it ceases to be grace! The whole essence of grace is that it is free and not dependent. Writing in the Tyndale New Testament Commentaries Series, Prof. R. V. G. Tasker says 'No other consideration influences (God) in this matter except His purpose to choose from the rest of His creatures a people who will be "holy, and without blemish before Him"'. Even people who somehow feel that they cannot come that far in their thinking find themselves quoting some of the great Bible verses which show it to be true:

Ephesians 2:8–9, for instance:—'For by grace are ye saved through faith; and that not of yourselves: it is the gift of God: not of works lest any man should boast'.

John 1:13 is another familiar verse, happily quoted by all Christians—and it says very clearly that our re-birth is '. . . not of blood, nor of the will of the flesh, nor of the will of man, but of God'.

2 Timothy 1:9 underlines the same truth when it says that God has '. . . saved us, and called us with an holy calling, not according to our works, but *according to His own purpose and grace*, which was given us in Christ Jesus before the world began . . .'

That leads us naturally to our next point:

Secondly, it is infinite in its beginning. In case that sounds like a contradiction in terms, let me explain! When we speak of birth, we have in mind a moment when life started—a birth-day as we call it. The same tends to be true spiritually. When we speak of a person becoming a Christian our thinking naturally centres around a *moment* of decision, of response, of faith, of commitment. It hinges on a date in the calendar, whether we know it or not. Now of course it is true that we have a decisive responsibility, but the whole truth goes deeper than that, and takes in a mystery and a miracle. The whole truth is that although our new birth happened in a moment of time, it was actually set in motion by God before time began. It is infinite in its beginning, because its beginning was in infinity, it began before time existed, it never had a beginning in terms of time. Scripture bears this truth out again and again. The prophet Jeremiah records God as saying 'Before I formed you in the womb I knew you, and before you were born I consecrated you; I appointed you a prophet to the nations' (Jeremiah 1:5 RSV). Notice how far the issue goes back—'Before I formed you . . .'! But we can go further back than that. The Apostle Paul says 'God chose you from the beginning to be saved, through sanctification by the Spirit and belief in the truth' (2 Thessalonians 2:13 RSV). Notice just what is being said here: that 'from the beginning' God chose the believer to salvation, and that salvation was worked out by the Holy Spirit separating the believer from the world and unto belief in the truth. There *was* a moment of faith, of belief, of commitment, but that was merely the outworking of God's eternal will before time began. Paul underlines this particular point—when he says that God 'chose us in Him before the foundation of the world' (Ephesians 1:4 RSV). Here is truth beyond our understanding, yet brought within our glad grasp by the Holy Spirit. Our new birth is infinite in its beginning.

Thirdly, it is infinite in its blessing. The verses we have just looked at are among the greatest in the Bible on the subject of Christian assurance. There are so many Christians, and particularly among those young in the faith, who find themselves in trouble time and time again over a question something like this—'Is it possible for me, at any time, to fall away so badly that I will be rejected by God, and, as it were, disenfranchised as far as the kingdom is concerned'? Now if the answer to that question is 'Yes', then we need to ask what it is that would cause this to happen. The answer, of course, would be sin. But if sin causes the believer to be lost, then every believer is lost every day of his life, and the argument is reduced to absurdity. The truth of the matter lies along an entirely different line. The Christian's eternal salvation depends not upon his choice of God, but upon God's choice of him. That is where it rests! So much evangelistic preaching, and counsel to those young in the faith, centres around *our* decision, *our* response, *our* faith, and I am sure that this is one reason why there are so many casualties in the work of evangelism today. It is also one of the reasons why there are so many Christians who spend an inordinate amount of time morbidly and introspectively concerned as to whether they are going to manage to hold on to the end and be eternally saved. They have never once got to grips with a glorious truth like this—'God chose us in Him before the foundation of the world'. Let me repeat, the Christian's eternal security does not depend on his choice of God, but on God's choice of him! How often John 6:37 is wrongly quoted in this connection! A professing convert is told to hold on to the phrase 'him that cometh to me I will in no wise cast out', whereas the real basis of assurance is in the first part of the verse, which says 'All that the Father giveth me shall come to me. . . .' The bedrock is 'the Father giveth'. In a covenant of redemption made between the Father and the Son before time began, every single one of God's elect people was put into a position where the infinite blessing of eternal salvation became theirs. The Christian's every blessing has its origin in eternity, and it is only when we grasp that that we can appreciate the Psalmist's words: '... the salvation of the righteous is of the Lord' (Psalm 37:39). When a man becomes a Christian he does so by God's intention and through God's initiative. Not without the preaching of the Gospel, of course; not without the offering of Christ; not without repentance and faith. But behind all of these, hidden in the reaches of eternity, is the purpose of God to save His people. We may be able to focus its operation in time, but we will only find its origin in eternity. The infinity of it!

2. *The instrument of the new birth.*—'with the Word of truth.

This is the same kind of phrase that Paul uses in Colossians 1:5, where he speaks of '... the hope which is laid up for you in heaven, whereof ye heard before in the word of the truth of the gospel', and in Ephesians 1:13 where he reminds his readers that their faith in Christ came 'after that ye heard the word of truth, the gospel of your salvation'. The Word of God is the instrument God uses to bring about the miracle of the new birth. God and His Word are so closely bound in this that the Psalmist can say 'Your word has revived me and given me life' (Psalm 119:50, The Amplified Bible).

The Bible gives a very rich collection of pictures about the power of God's Word in men's lives. Psalm 119:105 says 'Thy word is a lamp unto my feet and a light unto my path'—guiding, shining, showing the safe and sure pathway through life. In Jeremiah 5:14 God says to the prophet 'Because ye speak this word, behold I will make my words in thy mouth fire, and this people wood, and it shall devour them'—burning up all that cannot stand in the presence of God. Mark that verse if you are a preacher, a youth leader, a Sunday School teacher! Read it through again, and sense its promise and power. 'My words—thy mouth—fire'. Gimmicks may produce some kind of interest, but only God's word can produce ignition! Jeremiah 23:29. 'Is not my word like as a fire? saith the Lord; and like a hammer that breaketh the rock in pieces'?—smashing down man's futile rebellion against his Maker. Hebrews 4:12 'For the word of God is quick, and powerful, and sharper than any two-edged sword, piercing even to the dividing asunder of soul and spirit, and of the joints and marrow, and is a discerner of the thoughts and intents of the heart'—piercing through the veneer and excuses of the natural man and exposing the real heart of things. The longer I am a Christian, and the further I go into Christian service, the more convinced I become of the power that resides only and exclusively in the naked Word of God. I want to say something gently yet very carefully to all those concerned in evangelism, particularly in evangelism among young people, and perhaps even more particularly in evangelism among those with little or no religious or spiritual background at all, and it is this, I beg of you, in God's Name, never get into the situation where you have to evacuate the message in order to accommodate the method. Unless the Word of God is there, unless your work has the genuine ring of 'Thus saith the Lord', you cannot possibly claim any promise that God will bless your effort for Him. '. . . faith cometh by hearing, and hearing by the Word of God' (Romans 10:17). The instrument of it.

3. *The intention of the new birth.*—'that we should be a kind of firstfruits of His creatures'.

Verse 18 begins with the reason for our new birth—'of His own will'; now it ends by telling us the *purpose* for which we have been brought to spiritual life, the intention of the new birth—'that we should be a kind of firstfruits of His creatures'. Two words will help us to open up this phrase:

(a) *Dignity*. What a dignity there is about this description of God's people! In Exodus 19:5 God said to the people of Israel 'Now therefore, if ye will obey my voice indeed, and keep my covenant, then ye shall be a peculiar treasure unto me above all people. . . .' And then there is that extraordinary phrase in Ephesians 1:18 where we read about '. . . the riches of the glory of His inheritance in the saints'. A little earlier in that chapter we are told about the Holy Spirit being 'the earnest of *our* inheritance'—but here is a phrase that we would surely not dare to take upon our lips were it not there in the Bible; that God has great riches of inheritance, and those riches are His people—you and me included! We mean more to God than anything else in His creation. What a great dignity there is here! In Titus 2:14 Paul says that the Lord Jesus '. . . gave Himself for us that He might redeem us from all iniquity, and purify unto *Himself* a peculiar people (or as The Amplified Bible puts it '. . . to be a people peculiarly His own'), zealous of good works'. What a dignity! We have been chosen by God to be His own people, in a special way. We may be pilgrims here on earth, but we are not tramps! We are God's special people, and that gives us a great dignity.

(b) *Duty*. Privilege and responsibility are two sides of the same coin. You never have one without the other; never privilege without responsibility, and never responsibility without privilege. And just as nobody on earth could have a greater privilege than to be called and chosen to be a child of God, so no people on earth have greater responsibilities than Christians. We are privileged to be 'the firstfruits of His creatures' and that brings with it great responsibility. Let me put that responsibility in two phrases to close this chapter:

The first is this: *Gratitude of Heart*. Simply *because* we have been chosen, in spite of our sin and rebellion; ought we not to be grateful? We were chosen in Christ before the foundation of the world, before there was any kind of leaning towards God, any kind of desire for the Word, any kind of prayer by us or for us; before any of those things, God chose us in Christ. Ought that not to bring gratitude of heart?

The second is this: *Godliness of Life*. There is a lovely little phrase in Jeremiah 2:3 which says 'Israel was holiness unto the Lord and the firstfruits of His increase'. In certain versions of the Bible, the word 'and' is in italics, which means it was probably not in the original. There is no 'and' in this verse, and, if I can put it like this, there are not meant to be any 'ifs' or 'buts' either! 'Israel was holiness unto the Lord, the firstfruits of His increase'. The two together! God has chosen me, called me, saved me, secured me eternally; then let there be from my heart always an anthem of praise and gratitude. And let there be in my life that other accompanying anthem of holy living.

Thomas Manton once wrote 'Under the gospel there are no sin-offerings, only thank-offerings'. That's it! Nothing in our lives can ever be adequate as an offering for sin—and nothing is necessary, for Christ 'offered one sacrifice for sins for ever' (Hebrews 10:12) at Calvary. But all life, in every part, is meant to be a thank-offering, and in no way is God more properly thanked than by obedience.

Chapter 8

LIVE THE LIFE!

'Wherefore, my beloved brethren, let every man be swift to hear, slow to speak, slow to wrath: for the wrath of man worketh not the righteousness of God.' (James 1:19–20)

In our previous chapter, studying James 1:18, we were climbing in the rarefied heights of theology studying God's majestic, mysterious purposes before the foundation of the world. We only have to glance at the two verses quoted above to see that they refer to the plain issues of everyday life,—listening, getting angry, speaking. But although that seems to be a sudden, violent change, it is in fact a valid pattern. Although there may be much in our lives of unbiblical living, there is no such thing in the Bible as unpractical theology. There may be much in our lives that does not match up to the Bible, but there is nothing in the Bible that is not relevant to our lives. One of the places in the Bible which most wonderfully links the heights of theology with the plains of practical living is in John 13, recording the Last Supper. Let me quote you verse 3, in the Revised Standard Version—'Jesus knowing that the Father had given all things into His hands, and that He had come from God and was going to God. . . .' Now these are rarefied heights indeed! Just to read those words again, slowly, is to breathe in the very air of eternity and feel the touch of the eternal. And do you know what comes next? Look at verses 4 and 5—'(He) rose from supper, laid aside His garments, and girded Himself with a towel. Then He poured water into a basin, and began to wash the disciples' feet, and to wipe them with the towel with which He was girded'. From divinity to dirty feet, in three verses!

As we turn back to the Epistle of James and look at these two verses, let us be sure to remember that they follow immediately after verse 18, which speaks of the new birth. They are meant to deal with the outward expression of our inward experience.

I remember visiting a Bible College in France with two colleagues to speak to the students. Glancing over the shoulder of one of the students, one of us noticed that he had written these words: 'Conversion is the exteriorization of the experience of regeneration.' Now that is quite a mouthful—even in a Bible College!—and I would have thought that one could say the same thing in a much simpler way. Surely what the student meant was this: the new life is the outworking of the new birth. And that is a truth that the Bible states in one place after another. Here are two of the best known:

2 Corinthians 5:17—'Therefore if any man be in Christ, he is a new creature: old things are passed away; behold, all things are become new.' There it is, plain as daylight—the new birth, followed by the new life.

Ephesians 2: 8–9—'For by grace are ye saved through faith; and that not of yourselves: it is the gift of God: not of works, lest any man should boast'. There is the new birth, ours by grace through faith. But notice what comes next: 'For we are His workmanship, created in Christ Jesus unto good works, which God hath before ordained that we should walk in them'. We are *never* saved *by* good works, but we *are* saved *unto* good works.

While it is certainly true that good works without faith are vain and empty as far as salvation is concerned, it is equally true that any profession of faith that does not issue in good works is equally vain and empty. As somebody once put it, 'Holiness is the visible part of salvation'. After all, you cannot see faith, or mercy, or grace, or the new birth—but you can see holiness!

This of course is James's great burden, that belief and behaviour should go together. Bridging over from verse 18 with the phrase 'Wherefore, my beloved brethren' he touches in verses 19 and 20 on three places where the new life should be seen to express itself. Every Christian should be 'swift to hear', 'slow to speak', and 'slow to wrath'. Here, says James, are three things that should characterize the born-again believer.

1. *Readiness.*—'Swift to hear', or as The Amplified Bible puts it, 'a ready listener'.

In Mark 4:24 Jesus said 'Take heed *what* ye hear' and in Luke 8:18 He said 'Take heed therefore *how* ye hear'. There are quite clearly things the Christian should strive to avoid hearing, he should shut his ears, turn away, refuse to allow the story to be told, the gossip to be passed on, the error to be spread; but there are other things the Christian should have a readiness to hear and to listen. Let us just note two of these.

(1) *In worship.* In the context of worship, we should be 'swift to hear'.

(a) *In Public.* One supreme moment for the preacher is when he has a sense that God has given him a word to speak, and has given the people an ear to listen. What a moment that is! Perhaps only a preacher can really know what I mean, though perhaps listeners too recognize something of the hush of the Holy Spirit, the recognition that God has united speaker and listener in a way peculiarly his own. But how often is it otherwise! The average Christian in this country probably hears between 50 and 100 hours of preaching a year—but I wonder *how* he hears?

Jesus once said 'Every one to whom much is given, of him will much be required' (Luke 12:48 RSV). Some Christians sit week by week, Sunday by Sunday, under Biblical, evangelical ministry, and in a way that I certainly do not understand in detail, but is nevertheless real and personal, God is going to require that at their hands. They have the opportunity, the privilege, the ministry. How do they listen? How do they hear? It sometimes seems to me that in all the fever of new ideas and all the technology of Christian communication, and the sometimes bizarre experimentation with art forms in worship and evangelism we may just have lost sight of one thing, and that is the unique place that preaching occupies in the economy of God. The Apostle Paul asks '. . . how shall they hear without a preacher? . . .' (Romans 10:14). In 1 Corinthians 1:21 he says that '. . . it pleased God by the foolishness of preaching to save them that believe', and in Titus 1:3 he reminds his colleague that God '. . . manifested His Word through preaching . . .' All I want to ask here is this: If that is the kind of store God sets by preaching, if God puts preaching in that position, then how carefully, and seriously, we ought to listen? How often do we listen to preaching either as a duty or as a diversion? How often do we attend a place of worship with hearts solemnly and thoughtfully bowed in Samuel's eager attitude—'Speak, for Thy servant heareth'? (1 Samuel 3:10). How do *you* listen to a preacher? Casually? Critically? Beware of grieving the Holy Spirit here!

(b) *In Private.* I have never yet met a Christian who is completely satisfied with his devotional life. Perhaps that is a good thing! It is certainly not surprising, for though prayer is so vital, and should be spontaneous, in experience it sometimes proves the most difficult spiritual exercise of all. Satan's heaviest artillery is directed to the spot where a Christian prays, and it is perhaps here above all that we most often 'wrestle . . . against principalities, against powers' (Ephesians 6:12). Even so, some parts of prayer are at times not difficult. Praise, for instance. Surely no Christian has difficulty in finding something for which to praise the Lord. The Bible says that we should be 'Giving thanks always for all things' (Ephesians 5:20). Asking, too, is surely not basically difficult. Indeed the danger is that our prayer time sometimes turns into a spiritual shopping list. Confession should not be difficult either. He is in a low state of grace who finds that he has no weakness, waywardness or wickedness for which forgiveness is needed.

But in all these things *we* do the talking! *We* praise. *We* ask. *We* confess. The really difficult thing is to listen: we call our devotional periods 'Quiet Times', but is it not true that our Quiet Times are almost filled with the noise of our own voices from beginning to end? Would we not all be enriched if we would learn to listen?—to pray with meaning the hymnwriter's familiar words?—

'Speak Lord in the stillness, while I wait on Thee
Hush my heart to listen in expectancy.'

(2) *In Witness.* Just a word here, because this may not be the main thrust of James's words. Just as a good doctor is helped in his diagnosis by encouraging the

patient to talk, and by being a good listener, so in personal evangelism one of our most valuable instruments is the stethoscope of disciplined silence! Dr. William Barclay tells somewhere of a linguist of whom it was said, 'He could be silent in seven different languages'! Very few Christians possess the gift of being wisely silent. Think that one through!

Having said that a Christian should be characterized by readiness—'swift to hear'—James now goes on to say something quite different, namely that the Christian should be characterized by—

2. *Reticence.*—'let every man be . . . slow to speak'.

When all the exceptions and excuses have been made, and all the 'ifs' and 'buts' accommodated, the plain unvarnished truth is that, basically, we talk too much! It is reported that Disraeli once said about one of his contemporaries 'He was intoxicated with the exuberance of his own verbosity', and I am afraid that the sin of Disraeli's contemporary shows no sign of being eradicated, either among politicians or Christians! The two books in the Bible usually reckoned to be the most immediately practical are the Book of Proverbs (which someone cleverly called 'God's transistorized wisdom'!) and the Epistle of James, and it is surely important to notice that again and again they deal with speech, with the use of the tongue, and that when they do so they almost always warn us against using the tongue too rapidly, too readily. Here are some examples:

Proverbs 10:19 RSV—'When words are many, transgression is not lacking, but he who restrains his lips is prudent.'

Proverbs 17:27 RSV—'He who restrains his words has knowledge.'

Proverbs 21:21 RSV—'He who keeps his mouth and his tongue keeps himself out of trouble.'

Notice the verbs used to govern the tongue's use!—'restrains', 'keeps'. Here is the mark of the maturing Christian!

When we come to the Epistle of James, the verse we are now looking at is the first hint of a subject that he touches on again in verse 26, deals with in almost the whole of chapter 3, and comes back to in 4:11.

The Rabbis used to have a saying that went something like this—'We have two ears given us, and one tongue. Our ears are open and exposed; our tongue is walled in behind our teeth', and from that biological observation they drew a spiritual and practical conclusion! Without necessarily taking our doctrine from Rabbis' uninspired proverbs, I do feel that we ought to recognize that something we have perhaps treated very casually, is treated by the Holy Spirit very seriously. Have we ever really given sufficient weight to what Jesus said in Matthew 12:36?—'But I say unto you that every idle word that men shall speak, they shall give account thereof in the day of judgment'. In the light of that statement, we can never again take James's word lightly—'Let every man . . . be slow to speak'.

Let me sketch out three areas in which I believe this must be applied—

Firstly, we should be slow to speak about ourselves. As the father of five boys, I know that the mark of a child is self-centredness, whereas the mark of a developing character is interest in others. In the spiritual realm, one of the greatest tragedies is to see a growing Christian—and not infrequently one who is articulate and gifted—whose speech is dominated by the capital 'I'. It is the mark of a child to be self-centred. Let me put it another way. One of the greatest blessings of our lives comes when either through someone else's spoken or written ministry, or directly through the ministry of the Holy spirit, we are made to see that our life and our speech centres almost exclusively, altogether too much, around ourselves. It is a great moment when we realize, as somebody has put it, that we have too much ego in our cosmos!

Philippians 2:3 says 'Let nothing be done through strife or vainglory; but in lowliness of mind let each esteem other better than themselves'. Boastfulness is not becoming for a Christian. Breaking it down a little further, as far as speaking about ourselves is concerned, here are three things about which we ought not to boast:

What we are. Put in its simplest terms, we ought not to boast about the fact that we are Christians. When we were studying verse 18, we were thinking about the great dignity of being among those who are peculiarly the Lord's own people. What a wonderful position in which to be! We are the children of the King. We belong to the only true aristocracy in the world. Yet that is no reason why we should be proud, proud in a carnal, fleshly sense. In Romans 3, Paul comes towards the end of a crunching argument, showing that men are saved only on the basis of Christ's death on their behalf, and adds 'Where is boasting then?' (v. 27). If this is so, if God has concluded all men under sin, and yet in His discriminating love has laid the sins of His people on Christ at Calvary and then drawn them to Himself so that they are saved from their sin and become the children of God, then what room is there for boasting? The answer follows immediately—'It is excluded', or as The Amplified Bible puts it, 'excluded, banished, ruled out entirely'. I think it was Archbishop Temple who once said 'The only thing a man contributes to his salvation is the sin from which he needs to be saved'. Let us not allow the aristocracy of our spiritual status to lead to arrogance.

What we have. Let me remind you of an important principle we noted in studying verse 1. The Apostle Paul warns the Christians at Corinth against the dangers of going beyond Scripture in an assessment of those holding position in the church, and in the course of his argument he asks those two unanswerable questions, '. . . what have you that you did not receive? If then you received it, why do you boast as if it were not a gift?' (1 Corinthians 4:7 RSV). Do you see the point? What do you have in the way of gift, or ability, of grace, or material possessions, or spiritual resources, or influence, or power? Make a list of all those advantages, blessings and abilities that are yours but which you did not receive as a free gift from God. Surely the point is clear! Now if you did receive them, if they are gifts of God's grace, then why do you act and speak as if you did not receive them, but they were the outcome of your own skill and efforts? That is the thrust of what Paul is saying here. We ought not to boast about what we have.

What we do. In 1 Corinthians 9:16, Paul says 'For though I preach the Gospel, I have nothing to glory of; for necessity is laid upon me, yea, woe is unto me if I preach not the Gospel'. Here is the high point of his life's work, the greatest thing he ever did, yet he claims that in doing that he has nothing of which he can boast. That is why in Ephesians 3:8 he can say 'Unto me, who am less than the least of all saints, is this grace (*notice that!*) given, that I should preach among the Gentiles the unsearchable riches of Christ'. I suppose we could say that 'less than the least' is pretty poor grammar—but Paul happily murders the grammar in order to magnify the grace! I must leave you to work out the implications in your own life, but remember that any valid work you do for the Lord, however costly, however faithful, however effctive, however efficiently done, is still a 'grace given'. Don't boast about it! We should be slow to speak about ourselves.

Secondly, we should be slow to speak about others. Here we can pinpoint another common fault, and one a little more subtle than the one about which we have just been thinking. The boaster stands out. If a man is always talking about himself, his words very quickly give offence, but the attitude I now want to mention can more easily pass for knowledge, or wisdom, or intelligence. I mean the kind of person who must, just *must* give an opinion on every issue, a judgment on every situation, and a verdict on every person. They simply cannot let any subject come into the conversation without their contribution being made. They simply must have their say. Whether or not they know anything about the matter concerned is immaterial. They must give the definitive judgment on the situation, the issue or the person concerned. So much could be added here, but I want to touch on only one word, one of the most evil, sinister, crippling words in the Christian Church—criticism! I dare to say that we are all guilty at times of saying about other people things that are unkind, unjust, untrue, unfair, unloving.

Very simply, let me give you two reasons only why, as James says on a related issue in the third chapter of his letter, 'these things ought not so to be':

Because of the mischief it starts. The old story is told of the woman who after years of malicious tongue-wagging became convicted of her sin, and came to her Minister to ask his advice. He listened carefully to her story, and then said 'If you want a clear conscience, you must take a bag of goose feathers, go around the neighbourhood, and put a goose feather outside the door of every single person you have slandered.' Away she went, and, a long time later, returned to the Minister with an empty bag. 'I have done what you said' she reported, 'but I feel no better.' 'Ah no', the Minister replied, 'you have only done half the job. What you must now do is to go around and pick all the feathers up again.' Now it so happened that there was a high wind blowing that day, with the result that when the woman returned hours later her bag was still empty. Weary and dejected, she said sadly 'It's no good. I can't find a single feather. It was easy enough to put them down, but I can't get even one of them back again.' 'Precisely,' said the Minister, 'and in just the same way it was easy to scatter your words of criticism and rumour, but now that they have gone it is impossible to bring them back.'

The story may be quaint, but what a thrust there is in the application! The Bible has a terribly solemn word about this—'There are six things which the Lord hates, seven which are an abomination unto Him: haughty eyes, a lying tongue, and hands that shed innocent blood, a heart that devises wicked plans, feet that make haste to run to evil, a false witness who breathes out lies, and a man who sows discord among brothers' (Proverbs 6:16–19 RSV). God hates and abominates the sowing of discord among His people, and I would almost dare to say that you are a most unusual person if at some time and in some degree you have not been guilty, so in a very subtle way, perhaps, and apparently with honourable intentions, of sowing discord among the people of

God. Then beware of the mischief it starts! J. B. Simpson once said 'I would rather play with forked lightning than speak a reckless word against a servant of Christ'. Spoken words, like a sped arrow, are impossible to take back. Changing the picture, rumour spreads like wildfire, bringing hurt and harm to countless people in its wake. How wise that word in Proverbs 26:20—'Where no wood is, there the fire goeth out: so where there is no talebearer, the strife ceaseth'.

Because of the merit it suggests. I remember, when visiting the ruins of ancient Corinth, being struck by the size of the *bema*, the judgment seat, used by Gallio in the story recorded in Acts 18. As I stood there and looked up at this enormous stone mass I could not help thinking 'What a height he had to rise to in order to judge others.' And isn't the subtle, unconscious, terrible truth this—that when we are busy criticising, judging others, we are suggesting that we are above the things for which we are judging them? As E. Stanley Jones wrote somewhere 'You may dispense moral judgments so that by the very dispensing of them you judge yourself moral.' When we say a man is careless, do we not also mean that we are careful? When we say that a man is proud, we are suggesting that we are humble? When we criticize a man's meanness we suggest our generosity? When we say that a man is just a little astray theologically, are we not in fact saying that he does not agree with us?—and by implication suggesting that our view is the only right one? The story is told of the little Presbyterian child who said to his Anglican contemporary 'You are only miserable sinners, *we* are totally depraved'! Listen to a word from James— '. . . who are you that you judge your neighbour?' (James 4:12 RSV).

Because of the mischief it starts and because of the

merit it suggests we should be slow to speak about ourselves.

Thirdly, we should be slow to speak about the Lord. Yes, strange as it may sound, I mean just that!—in two spheres:

(a) *In public.* Now the Bible does say 'with the mouth confession is made unto salvation' (Romans 10:10) and Jesus did command 'Ye shall be witnesses unto me' (Acts 1:8), but all this must be seen in context, and I believe that our word here—'slow to speak'—has real application at this point. For instance, I think it is a wrong system that sends enquirers straight home from the counselling room to announce their 'salvation' to all and sundry. Surely it would be wiser to let the life speak before the lips? Again, I think there is a basic error in pushing young converts on to the public stage to give their testimony. Their place is the Bible Class, not the evangelistic platform. Again I think he is gravely in error who encourages every articulate young Christian to go into full-time ministry'. The ministry of the Word is a calling from God, not a cajoling by men, and my advice to any young man thinking about this issue would be this—do not dare to set a foot into the full-time ministry until it is impossible for you to do anything else, until with Paul you can cry '. . . necessity is laid upon me; yea, woe is unto me if I preach not the Gospel'! (1 Corinthians 9:16). And added to all these instances, or, rather, mixed into them all, is the deeper, more general truth concerning the awful responsibility of speaking about the Lord. It is terribly possible to take the Lord's Name in vain by speaking without reason, research or revelation—of speaking not because we have something to say but because we must say something! Be 'slow to speak' about the Lord in public.

(b) *In private*. Very simply, what I mean is that we must be careful in our private devotional life, not to let our prayers, or our praises, become a torrent of thoughtless words, with little regard for the majesty and magnificence of the One with whom we are communing. In the words of Ecclesiastes 5:2 'Be not rash with thy mouth, and let not thine heart be hasty to utter anything before God; for God is in heaven, and thou upon earth; therefore let thy words be few'. One of the great dangers of our grasp, our God-given grasp of the truth of justification by faith and by faith alone is that we might tend to become pally with the Deity. We are encouraged to speak freely with God, but not to speak flippantly. This takes us back to the earlier point in this verse, to the need to be 'swift to hear', to the need for quiet, submissive meditation, to the need to 'Be still, and know that I am God' (Psalm 46:10).

In public witness and in private worship, let us watch those words!

Now to the third point in this section, which we can hinge on the word.

3. *Reluctance*—'Let every man be . . . slow to wrath, for the wrath of man worketh not the righteousness of God'.

In these words, taking in the end of verse 19 and the whole of verse 20, we have a rule and a reason.

Firstly, the Rule—'Slow to wrath'—or, as it is put in The Amplified Bible 'slow to take offence and get angry'. Notice very carefully that it does *not* say 'Never be angry'! The word we are using to head this section is 'reluctance', not 'refusal'. The Bible encourages anger, but within very careful limits. In Ephesians 4:26 Paul says 'Be ye angry'—but he immediately adds 'and sin not. . . .' Psalm 97:10 says 'Ye that love the Lord, hate evil'. If you read Mark 3:5 and John 2:13–17 you will see that although Jesus was in all points without sin, He was not at all times without anger! Maybe this kind of righteous anger is a missing element in our preaching and debate, and living. There are issues in our society and churches about which we ought to be angry more often. We ought to feel, speak, protest. Yet this is a dangerous pathway. There must be reluctance in the question of the Christian being angry. The line between righteous anger and personal irritation is sometimes very thin. There is sometimes a very hazy border between defending principles and defending ourselves. Think twice; think three times; count up to ten; put everything possible in the way before you reach the position where it can be said about you 'He or she is angry because they are irritated, offended, they have been inconvenienced, they have been disagreed with, they have been criticized, they have been proved wrong, their personal wishes have been ignored, they have been outvoted'. Put everything you possibly can in the way to prevent you reaching the position where people can say that you are angry without a righteous cause. Thomas Manton once wrote—'Anger groweth not by degrees like other passions, but at her birth she is in her full growth. The heat and fury of it is at first, therefore the best cure is deliberation': Think about it! Before you get steamed up, or vent your spleen on a subject—think about it! 'Good sense makes a man slow to anger' (Proverbs 19: 11 RSV). If we would be angry and *not* sin, we must be angry at nothing *but* sin!

Here is the rule then—'let every man be . . . slow to wrath'.

Secondly, the Reason. 'For the wrath of man worketh not the righteousness of God'. The precise interpretation of this phrase hinges on the word 'worketh', which in fact has two possible meanings. Let us just glance at both, taking as headings the sense each meaning would give:

(a) *It does not practise it*. The wrath of man does not reproduce the righteousness of God. It is 'the wrath of man', earthy and carnal, not the outworking of God's nature in his life. A blazing, irrational, uncontrolled temper is not the kind of thing one expects to see in a person indwelt by One who is described as being 'merciful and gracious, slow to anger and plenteous in mercy.' (Psalm 103:8). One of C. H. Spurgeon's critics pointed out a drunkard to him and said 'Mr. Spurgeon, there goes one of your converts.' Spurgeon replied 'Well, he looks like one of mine; he is certainly not one of the Lord's'! Bad temper does not speak of the new life, nor of the righteousness of God.

(b) *It does not produce it*. The end product of anger is not the righteousness of God. It does not result in the righteousness God loves to see in our lives. Look again at Ephesians 4:26—'Be ye angry and sin not; let not the sun go down upon your wrath'. Now in this verse we have the two words 'angry' and 'wrath', and the second of these words is stronger than the first. It hints that wrath is not static. Anger festers, develops; it spawns ill-feeling, resentment, and sin of every kind. In James's own words it 'worketh not the righteousness of God'. Is there a convicting word there for you? Have you let the sun go down on your wrath? Perhaps you have let hundreds of suns go down! Are you holding out in unjustified anger against someone, another Christian? Then beware! That kind of behaviour neither practises nor produces the righteousness of God. And the positive answer? James himself gives it later on in his letter—'The fruit of righteousness is sown in peace of them that make peace' (James 3:18).

Chapter 9

BLUEPRINT FOR BLESSING—I

'Wherefore lay apart all filthiness and superfluity of naughtiness, and receive with meekness the engrafted word, which is able to save your souls'.
(James 1:21)

Although I have isolated this verse in order to look at it in a chapter on its own, it could well be taken as part of a section ending at verse 25. The whole section—verses 21–25, give what we could call a 'Blueprint for Blessing', ending as they do with the closing words of verse 25—'this man shall be blessed in his deed.'

Basically, these verses deal with the Christian's approach to the Bible, his appropriation of the Word of God. In verse 21, which we will look at in this chapter, we see two things—something we need to remove and something we need to receive. Let us look at those in turn:

1. *Something we need to remove.*—'wherefore lay apart all filthiness and superfluity of naughtiness'.

Perhaps the best way to examine this phrase closely will be to notice that it says three things about sin.

Firstly, it speaks of SIN'S DEFILEMENT—'wherefore lay apart all filthiness'.

The higher a man's state of grace, the more serious does he reckon sin to be. When you hear a man joking about sin, and treating sin casually, you are listening to a man who is in a lower state of grace than he ought to be!

To the unconverted man, sin is generally a trifle, to the carnal Christian it is often a trouble, but to the sensitive saint it is always a tragedy. What a difference! To one, a diversion; to the second, a difficulty; to the third, a disaster!

Be that as it may, the word James uses here is 'filthiness'. Now I suppose that generally we would link that particular word with moral impurity of some kind. Yet here, James may well be linking what he says in verse 21 with verses 19 and 20, (notice the 'wherefore' which begins verse 21), and if that is so then James is applying this word 'filthiness' to an unwillingness to listen, and the spirit of criticism and to unrighteous, unjustified anger. Far from passing those things over as being of minor importance, he does not hesitate to describe them as 'filthiness' in God's eyes. Of course he does widen the issue by saying 'all filthiness', and straight away we are reminded of Isaiah 64:6 where we are told that 'all our righteousnesses are as filthy rags'. Charles Wesley has the same clear recognition of sin's defilement in one of his hymns:

Purge me from every evil blot;
My idols all be cast aside;
Cleanse me from every sinful thought,
From all the filth of self and pride.

We have already noted that James is a great illustrator, and here he uses, as it were, a picture from the bathroom. He says that we are to 'lay apart all filthiness', and the phrase 'lay apart' is just the sort of thing you would say about taking off a dirty shirt or a soiled garment of any kind. This is quite a familiar kind of phrase in the Epistles, perhaps because it is so easily understood.

Here are some other places where we find it:

Colossians 3:8—'But now ye also *put off* all these; anger, wrath, malice, blasphemy, filthy communication out of your mouth'. Notice, in passing, that these are almost all sins of speech!

Hebrews 12:1—'Let us *lay aside* every weight; and the sin which doth so easily beset us'. The words 'lay aside' are exactly the same as the phrase 'lay apart' here in James 1:21.

1 Peter 2:1—'Wherefore *laying aside* all malice, and all guile and hypocrisies, and envies, and all evil speakings'—notice those sins of the tongue again!—'as new born babes desire the sincere milk of the word that ye may grow thereby . . .' Notice the similarity of context here, Peter going on immediately, as James does in verses 22–25, to the subject of receiving the Word of God.

Looking at these three scriptures together, there is another similarity in the language used—'put off', 'lay aside', 'laying aside'. What is more, notice also the consistent thoroughness of the work—'*all* these', *every* weight', '*all* malice', '*all* guile', '*all* evil speakings', and here in James 1:21 '*all* filthiness'. There must be a recognition that *every* sin is a defilement, an abomination in the sight of God. Never think lightly of sin. 'Fools make a mock at sin' (Proverbs 14:9). The casual word, the idle gossip, the bitter spirit—these things, says James, are 'filthiness'. Sin's defilement.

Secondly, SIN'S DEPTH. 'and superfluity of naughtiness'. Now the word 'superfluity' does not mean that which we can do without! It has the same root as the phrase used in the story of the feeding of the 4000 in Mark 8 where we read 'and they took up of the broken meat *that was left* seven baskets . . .' The phrase '*that was left*' is similar to the word 'superfluity' here in James 1:21. And what did it mean on that day when the 4000 were fed? When all these people had eaten, the grass must have been littered with crumbs and left-overs; but then, at the command of Jesus, they went carefully around and removed all traces that they had ever been eating there. Now do you see the application of James's word? Everything in the Christian's life that shows the presence of the old man, the old nature, must be got rid of as soon as it appears. Not just the obvious, gross sins, but every 'superfluity of naughtiness', every single outward sign and mark of the old nature's inward presence. Matthew Poole, the 17th Century commentator, has a telling phrase on this. He says 'That is said to be superfluous or redundant which is more than should be in a thing; in which respect all sin is superfluous'. Do you see his point? 'Superfluous' means anything there ought not to be. More than there should be. And as far as sin in the Christian's life is concerned, that means that all of it is superfluous!

But why does sin appear in the Christian? Why does there have to be this never-ending battle? Why this constant vigilance? Why the many Scriptures bearing on this subject? Isn't the whole question of sin dealt with at conversion? Isn't the old nature removed there and then? No! The old, sinful nature remains, hidden deep in his personality. That is why I have called this section '*Sin's depth*'. There is a depth of sin in us all that we need to recognize and unless constant action is taken the signs of its presence will appear, even in the life of the most mature among us. That is true for *every* Christian, even for those who do not believe it! A woman once came to her Minister and said 'I want you to know that all sin has been completely eradicated from my nature'.

He carefully replied 'Really! Then you must be very proud.' Falling headlong into the trap, she cried 'Oh yes, I am'!

The depth of it! The Amplified Bible translates 'superfluity of naughtiness' by the phrase 'the rampant outgrowth of wickedness'. Here, the picture changes from the bathroom to the garden. The evil roots are there, and given the slightest opportunity they will send up the shoots and branches of sin. He is an unwise and unprepared Christian who will not recognize solemnly and seriously before God the depth of indwelling sin in the human heart. The hymnwriter has it exactly right in these well-known words:

'And none, O Lord, have perfect rest,
For none are wholly free from sin.
And those who fain would serve Thee best
Are conscious most of wrong within'.

Sin's defilement, sin's depth, and now

Thirdly, SIN'S DAMAGE. This is not openly stated here, but it is obviously inferred, because before coming on to the question of receiving the Word of God, James first of all deals with removing certain things which prevent the Word of God being properly and helpfully received. He is concerned to prepare the ground for the seed of the Word. It is said that the word 'filthiness', is derived from the Greek word 'rupos' which when used medically, means 'wax in the ear'. And when James says 'lay apart all filthiness' he would mean anything that stops us hearing, receiving and understanding the Word of God. A little while ago, I was leading family prayers at home, and we were reading together part of the fifth chapter of Acts. We reached the incident where the Pharisee named Gamaliel came to the defence of the disciples, and I asked one of my little boys what it was that Gamaliel did. With a worried frown, he scoured the Bible-reading notes we were using at the time, looking for the magic word. Sensing his difficulty, I tried to help him out by spelling the word—'d-e-f-e-n-d-e-d'. 'Got it'!, junior blurted. 'Gamaliel deafened the disciples'! Beware of anything that deafens you to the Bible! Sin could do no greater damage than that. Not until I was studying this passage did I take a slow and serious look at Luke 9:44 'Let these sayings sink down into your ears'. Do you see the point? Get rid of everything that becomes, as it were, wax in the ears, everything that prevents you hearing and understanding the Word of God. These things must be recognized, regretted and removed.

How can this be done? Here are two open secrets.

(1) *Confess them in God's presence*. It is a wonderful principle to remember that whatever we cover, God uncovers, and whatever we uncover, God covers. The Bible makes that plain—'He who conceals his transgressions will not prosper, but he who confesses and forsakes them shall have mercy' (Proverbs 28:13 RSV). Whatever we seek to hide from God, whatever we gloss over and tolerate, God exposes and shows us its folly. Conversely, whatever we uncover, whatever we recognize and confess and name before Him as sin, He covers with the precious blood of Christ. Remember that 1 John 1:9 was originally written to Christians—'If we confess our sins, He is faithful and just to forgive us our sins and to cleanse us from all unrighteousness'.

(2) *Conquer them in God's power*. Of course we cannot conquer sin, even the smallest sin, in our own power. Nor is the answer to 'Let go and let God'—which can be among the most dangerous of doctrines. The

answer is active, not passive. It is being 'more than conquerors through Him that loved us' (Romans 8:37). The Christian's victory is when *he* fights in *God's* strength!

2. *Something we need to receive.*—'and receive with meekness the engrafted word, which is able to save your souls'.

Perhaps the simplest way of opening up this phrase is to notice that it answers four basic questions about the Christian reading or 'receiving' the Word of God. What should he receive? And how should he receive it? And where? And why? The answers are all here!

(a) *What?*—'receive . . . the . . *Word*'. I suppose that one of our commonest faults is that we are bad readers, that we read so little. If that is not universally true, then perhaps our fault is in *what* we read. Even if we lay aside all the books and newspapers and magazines and articles and comments that we read outside of a purely religious context; if we put all of these on one side and we are left alone with our purely religious reading, now *what* do we read? Well, we read books and newspapers and magazines and articles and comments! I wonder what a shattering equation we would get if some unseen computer was working out how much of our reading, proportionately, is the Word of God itself? Beware of becoming an avid reader of books about the Bible to the neglect of the Bible itself! Beware of becoming a great reader of devotional books and commentaries, and missionary books and magazines, but not of the Word itself. The promise of the Holy Spirit to interpret the Word of God is as real to you, and can be as meaningful to you as to the greatest commentator and expositor the world has ever known. God knows your every need, and is able to apply His Word directly to your individual need and circumstances without any human assistance whatever. He is able to do that! That is not to say that He does not use other means, but it should warn us of the danger of relying upon them. Beware of being a reader of everything else except the Bible.

(b) *How?*—'*. . . receive with meekness*'. The word 'meekness' has been called 'the untranslatable word'. Even The Amplified Bible seems unsettled, using three words 'humble, gentle, modest'. It seems to me that in the context of our approach to the Bible, the word is trying to say something like this—openness, a willingness to hear whatever God has to say without any preconceived ideas of our own. There is a lovely illustration of this in Acts 10, the story of the conversion of Cornelius. The Apostle Peter, staying at the time at Joppa, received an urgent message from Cornelius, a Roman centurion living in Caesarea. Convinced by God's explanation of his extraordinary rooftop vision that this was a call to preach the Gospel to the Gentiles, Peter travelled quickly to Caesarea, where he was enthusiastically met by Cornelius with the words '. . . thou hast well done that thou art come. Now therefore are we all here present before God, to hear all things that are commanded thee of God' (Acts 10:33). What a thrill for Peter! What a moment for any preacher!—when those who sit before him do so with such an openness, such a readiness, to hear 'all things that are commanded . . . of God'! And that is the spirit in which we ought to approach the Word of God. We should say, as it were, 'Lord, I am here, and'—reverently, we could add this—'I am glad that You have come, and I am ready to hear whatever You have to say to me from the Word. *Whatever* you have to say—be it a word of cheer, of chastening or of challenge'. That is the right spirit.

That is *how* we should receive the Word. Yet so often we come so differently. Isn't it true that too often we come embroiled in our backgrounds? Isn't it true that too often we come to the Bible wearing the blinkers of our own pet theological school of thought, or doctrinal tradition. We will not allow the whole of the Word of God to speak to us; only those parts which plainly agree with our ideas or convictions. If you put a certain kind of filter over the lens of a camera, certain features of the sky or landscape will stand out more than others. Isn't it true that we sometimes come to the Bible wearing the filter of our own preconceived ideas, so that only the parts we emphasize in our thinking will stand out from the page? Beware of this. 'Receive with meekness'.

(c) *Where?—'the engrafted word'*. The adjective here literally means 'implanted'. I am no horticulturalist, but I would have thought that, by and large, sowing on the surface is only for trivial things. You cannot grow oak trees in window boxes! The Amplified Bible translates this word 'implanted and rooted in your hearts' and I am sure that that helps us to get the right picture—the whole personality wrapping itself around the seed of the Word, burying it deeply into the soil of one's mind and spirit. The Apostle Paul uses this kind of picture in 1 Corinthians 3:9 when he says 'Ye are God's husbandry', and The Amplified Bible translates the word 'husbandry' like this—'God's garden and vineyard and field under cultivation'. The seed of God's Word is meant to sink deeply into the soil of your soul, so that it can germinate effectively and produce the fruit of the Spirit in your life.

(d) *Why?—' . . . which is able to save your souls'*. 'But wait a minute,' I can hear somebody objecting, 'surely this is written to Christians? Are they not already saved?' Well, that depends upon what you mean by 'saved'! The Bible speaks of a Christian being 'saved' in three different senses. Let us just note them in passing so that we can get into accurate focus the point James is making.

Firstly, there is the initial possession.—Ephesians 2:8 'By grace are ye saved'. That speaks of a once-for-all, unrepeatable, unalterable experience, the thing that happens the moment a person puts his trust in the Lord Jesus Christ. This marks the beginning of Christian experience. The initial possession.

Secondly, there is the gradual progress—1 Corinthians 1:18 'The preaching of the cross is to them that perish foolishness, but to us which are saved it is the power of God'. Now the verb 'saved' here is in the present tense—it could literally be translated 'being saved'. In this sense, being saved is a gradual process, something being hammered out on the anvil of a Christian's developing experience, a maturing, refining, growing work which begins at conversion and will continue until his dying day. The gradual progress.

Thirdly, there is the final prospect.—Romans 5:9 'Much more then, being now justified by His blood, we *shall be saved* from wrath through Him'. This sense of being 'saved' is not part of a Christian's testimony to the past, nor of his experience of the moment, but it is a certainty in every Christian's future—he 'shall be saved from wrath through Him'. It is the final, glorious, heavenly, prospect to which all else is prologue.

Now I may not have all the scholars on my side, but I believe that when James speaks of the engrafted Word saving our souls, he is referring to 'saved' in the second of these three senses. In an earlier study we noticed the

Apostle Peter's word '. . . desire the sincere milk of the word that ye may grow thereby' (1 Peter 2:2), and to that we could add Paul's farewell word to the Elders of Ephesus—'I commend you to God, and to the Word of His grace, which is able to build you up' (Acts 20:32). What a need there is in our churches, in our young people's fellowships, and in our individual Christian lives for this ministry of building up! My experience of work among young people convinces me that there are multitudes of Christian teenagers in our country who have been converted for several years and yet who would be very hard pressed to quote even 20 verses from the Bible with the accurate reference. One of the root meanings behind the word 'salvation' is the word 'health', and I have never yet met a weakly Christian whose difficulties did not include the lack of disciplined, devoted reading of the Word of God.

Where do you stand on this particular issue? You may have been a Christian for some time, perhaps for years. You are busy, active in the Lord's service. Yet in your own inmost heart, in the place where their can be no pretence, you know that you are nowhere near the state of maturity and blessing which ought to be yours. Is this because the Word of God is not being implanted in your heart? And is it not being implanted into your heart because you are not approaching it with meekness, with openness, with willingness that God should speak in any way that He chooses? And are you not doing that because there are so many other things—so many legitimate things—that are crowding out the Bible? Things that need, as we saw earlier in this chapter, to be removed, so that the Word of God can be received, and your soul saved, made healthy, built up, matured, nourished in all the goodness of God. It will be a turning point in your Christian experience if, by the grace of God, you begin in a new way to 'lay aside all filthiness and superfluity of naughtiness, and receive with meekness the engrafted word which is able to save your souls', making the words of A. C. Barham Gould's hymn your constant prayer:

'May the Word of God dwell richly
In my heart from hour to hour,
So that all may see I triumph
Only through His power!'

Chapter 10

BLUEPRINT FOR BLESSING—II

'But be ye doers of the Word, and not hearers only, deceiving your own selves.

For if any be a hearer of the Word, and not a doer, he is like unto a man beholding his natural face in a glass:

For he beholdeth himself, and goeth his way, and straightway forgetteth what manner of man he was.

But whoso looketh into the perfect law of liberty, and continueth therein, he being not a forgetful hearer, but a doer of the work, this man shall be blessed in his deed'.

(James 1:22–25)

These four verses carry on the subject which James introduced at the end of verse 21, the matter of receiving the Word of God, and if you look at them carefully you will see that they indicate two approaches men have to the Bible. Both sections are introduced by the word 'But . . .'. The first, at verse 22, begins 'But be ye doers of the word and not hearers only . . .', and is an approach characterized by *casual observance*. The second, at verse 25, begins 'But whoso looketh into the perfect law of liberty and continueth therein . . .' and is an approach characterized by *careful obedience*. Let us look at each of them in detail.

1. *Casual observance*—'But be ye doers of the word and not hearers only, deceiving your own selves. For if any be a hearer of the word, and not a doer, he is like

unto a man beholding his natural face in a glass: For he beholdeth himself, and goeth his way, and straightway forgetteth what manner of man he was.

The heart of this approach could really be summed up in two words from verse 22—'hearers only'. James does not condemn a person for reading his Bible, for being a hearer of the Word, but for being a hearer *only*. His concern is that there is the kind of person whose approach to the Bible goes no further than being a 'hearer of the Word' (v. 23).

Having got the general picture we need to separate the two strands woven into these verses:

Firstly, there is a simple comparison.—'For if any be a hearer of the Word, and not a doer, he is like unto a man beholding his natural face in a glass' (v. 23). James is back at his picture-language again! He says that a man who treats the Bible in a casual way is 'like unto a man beholding his natural face in a glass'. Let us look at some word meanings here, beginning at the end of the sentence.

A 'glass' quite simply means a mirror. There is no problem there. But the rather odd expression 'natural face' means literally 'the face with which he was born'. Now of course what we see in our bathroom mirror is not identical morning by morning, and it is therefore not *exactly* the same face with which we were born. The texture, the contours, the size, change gradually over the years. The point of the phrase here is that the mirror shows exactly what is there, unwelcome though the truth may sometimes be! The word 'beholding' is a little tricky, for although it is a strong word, the whole drift is to indicate a casual, superficial look—what we might call 'a look and a promise'! As Professor R. V. G. Tasker says, 'He tends to look at his face often, but never for very long'! Be that as it may, I think James's message is clear. Here is the simple comparison. A man gets up in the morning, dashes to the mirror, swishes the razor and flannel over his face, throws the comb through his hair, gulps his breakfast and dashes for the train—by which time he has completely forgotten the details of what his face looked like a few minutes earlier! Here, says James, is a simple comparison. The Christian he has in mind comes to his Bible, hurriedly dashes through a passage, skims over somebody else's pre-digested notes, bows his head for a moment of prayer, and then is off into the mad whirl of business and busyness—with as little detailed understanding of what he has read as the other man had knowledge of the precise delineations of his face.

Does that find you out? Is your own personal approach to the Bible one of casual observance?

It is only a step away to say that this same, fatal approach is often true in the public reading of scripture. There are times when I have felt that the Bible was being read with as little preparation as the notices, and with even less understanding. I hesitate to use the following illustration, because of the part I have in it, but I do so as much as a constant reminder to my own heart as a challenge to yours. When I was first appointed as a Lay Reader in the Church of England, attached to Holy Trinity Church, Guernsey, there were two other, more senior, Lay Readers on the staff, with the result that on most Sundays the responsibilities at morning and evening could be very well shared out. It so happened that the Vicar, who was of course in charge of our duties, almost always asked me to read the Lessons, so that this became almost a standing arrangement. We were following a Lectionary, which meant that the Lessons were set out for a whole year in advance. My wife and I lived in a small flat at the time, and I can vividly remember my Sunday morning routine. Immediately after breakfast I would go into the bedroom, lock the door, and begin to prepare for reading the Lesson that morning. After a word of prayer I would look up the Lesson in the Lectionary, and read it carefully in the Authorized Version, which we were using in Church. Then I would read it through in every other version I had in my possession, in order to get thoroughly familiar with the whole drift and sense of the passage. Next I would turn to the commentaries. I did not have many in those days, but those I had I used. I would pay particular attention to word meanings and doctrinal implications. When I had finished studying the passage in detail, I would go to the mantelpiece, which was roughly the same height as the lectern in the church, and prop up the largest copy of the Authorized Version I possessed. Having done that, I would walk slowly up to it from the other side of the room, and begin to speak, aloud—'Here beginneth the first verse of the tenth chapter of the Gospel according to St. John' (or whatever the passage was). Then I would begin to read, aloud, the portion appointed. If I made so much as a single slip of the tongue, a single mispronunciation, I would stop, walk back across the room, and start again, until I had read the whole thing word perfect, perhaps two or three times. There were times, as my wife would tell you, when I emerged from that bedroom with that day's clean white shirt stained with perspiration drawn from the effort of preparing one or two passages of Scripture to be read in the church. Does that sound like carrying things too far? Then let me add this—and I know this to be true because it was reported to me—there were times when after the reading of the Lesson, people wanted to leave the service there and then and go quietly home and think over the implications of what God had said to them in His Word.

Now you know why I hesitated to tell the story, but I praise God for impressing upon me the importance of not having this casual observance that characterizes so much of our approach to the Bible. Surely we do God a disservice when we dare to treat His sacred and solemn Word in a casual, offhand way. The marginal reading of part of Jeremiah 48:10 says 'Cursed be he that doeth the work of the Lord negligently . . .' I am afraid that James's simple comparison is too often true.

Secondly, notice a sad conclusion. In fact, as we thread our way through these verses, we can pick out three sad conclusions experienced by the man who has this casual approach to Scripture:

(a) *He thinks, but he does not know.*—'. . . deceiving your own selves' (v. 22).

The Bible has a great deal to say about being deceived. It says we can be deceived by Satan—it describes him as 'the deceiver of the whole world' (Revelation 12:9 RSV). It says we can be deceived by other people: Jesus warned us to 'Take heed that no man deceive you' (Matthew 24:4). But here the expression is 'deceiving your own selves', surely a reminder of the words in Jeremiah 17:9 where we are told that 'the heart is deceitful above all things, and desperately wicked . . .'. Now it is important to notice that the word 'deceiving' here in James 1:22 stems from a verb meaning 'to be deceived by false reasoning'. In context, it may mean the approach that says because one thing has happend, something else automatically follows. The application would therefore be this: 'I have read my Bible, said my prayers, had my Quiet Time, so everything is fine. I have gone through the process, so I can assume the progress.' Now that is false reasoning!—and its implications are so deep that it may be the most serious issue we touch on in the whole Epistle of James. It is perilously possible to deceive ourselves into thinking that progress has been made or that an issue has been satisfactorily dealt with, when we have learned a new truth, heard a fine sermon or (and this especially to preachers and teachers) when we have taught the truth about a certain subject. Beware this terrible danger! I am sure that we have often come away from a service, a rally, or a Bible Study saying 'I have really learned something tonight', but I wonder how often we could also have added 'From that moment, that particular part of God's Word entered into the bloodstream of my life and changed it for God and for good'? What a difference there is between thinking and knowing! There is a difference between reading a menu and eating a meal! There is a difference between reading a prescription and taking the medicine! There is a difference between reading the Bible and growing in grace! How easy it is to be deceiving our selves on this issue!

(b) *He looks but he does not see*—'he beholdeth himself . . . and straightway forgotteth what manner of man he was' (v. 24). There used to be a well-known watch advertisement which asked two questions: The first was something like this—'Are the numerals on your watch Roman or Arabic or some other kind?' Having discovered this, one then read the second question which was '*Without looking at your watch again*, can you say what the exact time is?' As the advertisers expected, I couldn't!—and neither, I suspect, could most of those who read the advertisement! I had looked at the face of my watch just a moment before, yet did not see the most vital truth that was in front of my eyes and on the face of the dial. I am sure the application is obvious! Here is another sad conclusion of a casual observance of the Word of God. We look at the words, but we do not actually see them. Or, to put it more accurately, we look at the Scriptures long enough to see the words but not deep enough to see the truth. Changing the picture completely, we come to a Book which is described as being 'sharper than any two-edged sword' (Hebrews 4:12) yet we often manage to get away without a scratch! It is possible to be Bible hardened, Quiet Time hardened, to forget what the Bible is essentially meant to be and to be doing, and to become dulled and deadened as to the vitality and virility of God's Word. In Isaiah 66:2 God says '. . . to this man will I look, even to him that is poor and of a contrite spirit *and trembleth at my word*'. Telling the story of his vision, Daniel cries 'And when He had spoken this word unto me I stood trembling' (Daniel 10:11). When did we last do that? How we need to follow the example of those to whom Paul wrote —'And we also thank God constantly for this, that when you received the word of God which you heard from us, you accepted it not as the word of men, but as what it really is, the word of God, which is at work in your believers' (1 Thessalonians 2:13 RSV). Much too often a Christian receives the Word quite differently —he thinks, but he does not know; he looks but he does not see.

(c) *He hears but he does not act.*—'. . . he goeth his own way . . .' (v. 24). Surely this is the saddest conclusion of all! Notice the 'his'! J. B. Phillips paraphrases these words '. . . he goes on with what he was doing.' The rich young ruler whose story is recorded in Mark 10:17–22, was rather like that. He came to the right Person, with the right question, got the right answer, but went the wrong way—his own way! It is tragically possible to do that. I remember a young man of 23 telling me once that he had spent a total of ten years in prisons and Approved Schools. On one occasion the authorities had punished him by ordering him to write out Psalm 121 a hundred times. He went on to tell me that even this had made no difference to him, and I replied 'No, but had you believed and obeyed those words just once you would have been converted, a changed man'! Hearing or reading the Word of God is vitally important, but not totally so. There is something else needed. The writer to the Hebrews puts this so clearly when he says of some people '. . . the word preached did not profit them, not being mixed with faith in them that heard it' (Hebrews 4:2). Many had heard, but not all had profited. The hearing needed to be followed by faith, a faith implying committed obedience. Does your Bible reading stand that test? It is vital that it should! Beware of being in the first group, whose Bible reading is characterized by casual observance.

2. *Careful obedience.*—'But whoso looketh into the perfect law of liberty, and continueth therein, he being not a forgetful hearer, but a doer of the work, this man shall be blessed in his deed' (v. 25).

Notice how the word 'But' introduces us to a person vastly different to his approach. The man typified in the first section was 'a hearer of the word and not a doer' (v. 23): this man is 'not a forgetful hearer, but a doer of the work' (v. 25). The whole verse says two things, in a most clear and helpful way:

Firstly, The Duty of Looking Attentively—'But whoso looketh into the perfect law of liberty and continueth therein'. That phrase seems to me to suggest three things that should characterize the Christian's Bible Study.

(a) *Discernment*. The Word of God is described as 'the perfect law of liberty', and that statement alone could form the basis of a whole series of Bible Studies! Let us simplify it like this. As we saw in an earlier study, the law of God is perfect, and if a man kept the law in every detail he would be in perfect spiritual harmony with God, justified in God's sight because of his own obedience. But we also know that all men have failed. Yet the Christian believer is in the wonderful position in which all of Christ's obedience to the law is credited to him. If only this could be got across—especially to those young in the faith. This issue of being a Christian is not simply and only and exclusively a matter of having our past sins forgiven and blotted out. That is only a part of one side of the truth. Of course it is wonderfully true that the believer's sin was taken upon Christ and dealt with in His death on the Cross; but it is no less wonderfully and just as importantly true that all of Christ's obedience to the law is credited to the believer. That is why Christ is prophetically described in Jeremiah 23:6 as 'The Lord our Righteousness'. What could never be done by the Christian has been done for him. It is at this precise point that we find the practical application of that glorious truth that the Lord Jesus Christ was 'in all points tempted like as we are yet without sin' (Hebrews 4:15). The sinlessness of the Lord Jesus Christ is an essential part of God's amazing provision that makes a Christian acceptable before Him. As Paul says in Romans 10:4, 'Christ is the end of the law for righteousness to everyone that believeth'. The believer is set free from the place where the law has any power to condemn him. Paul's own testimony was this—'. . . the law of the Spirit of life in Christ Jesus has set me free from the law of sin and death' (Romans 8:2).

But there is another contingent truth which brings us near to the heart of what Jesus is saying here. The Christian is not only free from bondage to the law, he is also free from his natural hatred of it—he now finds that he delights in what he once detested. The law is not now a burdensome outward set of rules and regulations imposed by a distant Stranger who threatens extermination for every infringement. The law is now something which finds a responsive chord in the heart of the believer. In the Psalmist's words 'I delight to do Thy will, O my God, yea Thy law is within my heart'. (Psalm 40:8). The Amplified Bible's version of Psalm 119:32 puts it even more expressively—'I will not merely walk, but run the way of Your commandments when You give me a heart that is willing'. Remember that the point we are making here is that the Christian should have *discernment* in his reading of the Bible; and the application of what I have just been saying is that that discernment should include an understanding of what the law is, of where he stands in relation to it, and of his potential obedience to it. The Christian is free to obey the law, and to know the blessing that comes from obedience. This is not liberty without law, nor law without liberty. It is 'the law of liberty'. Do you see the difference? Discernment! That is one thing that should characterize our reading of God's Word. Here is a second:

(b) *Depth*—'. . . whoso looketh . . .'. This word 'looketh' has a common root with a phrase used in Luke 24:12, part of the resurrection story, where we read

'Then arose Peter, and ran into the sepulchre, *and stooping down*, he beheld the linen clothes by themselves, and departed, wondering in himself at that which was come to pass'. With no time here to paint the picture in detail, we can surely recognize something of what was at stake at that moment: the deity of Christ, the whole of Peter's own future, the existence of the Church as a body of believers, all hinged on this issue. Imagine Peter's concern to look carefully, to be sure, to make no mistake, especially in the imperfect light of early morning. '. . . and stooping down . . .' is the Bible's way of describing what he did, and we can be sure that the phrase describes not a glance but a gaze, a thorough, careful scrutiny of every nook and cranny. When James uses another tense of the same verb to describe the right kind of Bible reader, the implication is obvious! I remember once reading that in the Johannesburg area of South Africa there are at least 55 gold mines, some of them nearly 12,000 feet deep. Men were not only prepared to go that tremendous depth into the earth, but to bring up to the surface up to four tons of ore in order to produce one ounce of gold. Do you remember what David said about the Word of God?—'The law of the Lord is perfect, converting the soul: the testimony of the Lord is sure, making wise the simple. The statutes of the Lord are right, rejoicing the heart: the commandment of the Lord is pure, enlightening the eyes. The fear of the Lord is clean, enduring for ever: the judgments of the Lord are true and righteous altogether. *More to be desired are they than gold, yea, than much fine gold:* sweeter also than honey and the honeycomb. Moreover by them is thy servant warned: and in keeping of them there is great reward'. (Psalm 19:7–11). The Bible is our final written authority in all matters of faith and practice. We need to 'stoop down' to it, to apply ourselves to it with intimate care, and to pray for the Holy Spirit's help in piercing beneath the surface in order to discover and discern its deeper truths. Discernment—'the perfect law of liberty'. Depth—'. . . . whoso looketh . . .' But there is something else here—

(c) *Discipline.* '. . . and continueth therein . . .', or as The Amplified Bible puts it, '. . . is faithful to it and perseveres in looking into it'. When the Apostle Paul visited Athens there were those who described him as 'this babbler'. (Acts 17:18). This word 'babbler' translates the Greek word *spermologos*, a little grain-eating bird that flitted here and there, picking up minute trifles and titbits, but never staying anywhere long enough to get its beak into anything solid. The fact that Paul's critics said that about someone so disciplined in his application and so massive in his intellect, was a mark of their own ignorance of course. But would the description fit you? Are you satisfied with a few verses or phrases here and there, a few comforting clichés, a thought for the day? Is your Bible study a matter of fits and starts? Or is it marked by the determined discipline which God promises to reward? George Duncan once wrote somewhere 'God does not reveal the deep things of the Spirit to the casual Christian who drops in for a chat'. Of course I am not suggesting that you are able to spend several hours in reading and meditation before breakfast every morning—but what about the whole structure of your Bible Study? Well, that is the first thing that is made clear in this verse, *the duty of looking attentively.* But there is a second thing—

The Delight of Living Accordingly—'. . . he, being not a forgetful hearer, but a doer of the work, this man shall be blessed in his deed'. Notice very carefully that it is 'in his deed' that this man is 'blessed'. This is the whole thrust of the phrase. The man is not said to be blessed automatically in proportion to the amount of Biblical knowledge he accumulates. The blessing comes with his obedience to the revealed will of God. That is a truth so basic, and upon which the Scripture insists so often, that we must just spend a moment to underline it—

Psalm 19:9 and 11—'The judgments of the Lord are true and righteous altogether . . . and in *keeping* of them there is great reward'.

Psalm 106:3—'Blessed are they that *keep* judgment and that *doeth* righteousness at all times'.

Psalm 119:2—'Blessed are they that *keep* His testimonies . . .'.

Luke 11:28—'. . . blessed are they that hear the word of God and *keep* it'.

John 13:17—'If ye know these things, happy are ye *if ye do them*'.

Revelation 22:7—'. . . blessed is he that *keepeth* the sayings of the prophecy of this book'.

Notice the insistence on keeping, or obeying the Word of God, and not just on knowing it! Notice something else too: in none of these verses is there any indication of *how* a man is blessed when he is obedient. I believe there is a reason for this, namely that when a man comes to the Word with an open, willing heart, and comes from it with a submissive, obedient will, then God blesses him in every part of his life. He will be blessed in his home, in his family life, in his work, in his Christian service, and in the inner recesses of his own soul. A man once came home from a Church service much earlier than expected. 'You are early,' said his wife. 'Is the sermon done already?' 'No,' he replied, 'It is preached. It is going to begin to be done now!'

That is it! The delight of living accordingly. And the finest summary of it all is given in the opening words of the Psalms:

> *'Blessed is the man who walks not in the counsel of the wicked, nor stands in the way of sinners, nor sits in the seat of scoffers; but his delight is in the law of the Lord and on His law he meditates day and night. He is like a tree planted by streams of water, that yields its fruit in its season, and its leaf does not wither. In all that he does, he prospers.'*
>
> (Psalm 1:1–3 RSV)

Chapter 11

FALSE AND TRUE RELIGION

'If any man among you seem to be religious, and bridleth not his tongue, but deceiveth his own heart, this man's religion is vain. Pure religion and undefiled before God and the Father is this, To visit the fatherless and widows in their affliction, and to keep himself unspotted from the world.'

(James 1:26–27)

To many people, one of the dullest words in the English language is the word 'religion'. It seems to speak of dull, dreary discipline, a morbid mixture or what J. B. Phillips somewhere calls 'rites and robes, bells and smells'. And when these people read Paul's testimony that as a Pharisee he had lived 'according to the strictest party of our religion' (Acts 26: 5 RSV), their worst impressions seem to be confirmed.

These two closing verses of the first chapter of the Epistle of James deal with the subject of religion, and in them the Apostle James, down-to-earth as ever, shows the difference between the caricature of religion which some people hold and the true expression of living faith in God. In other words these verses tell us something about false religion and something about true religion.

1. *False religion condemned*—'If any man among you seem to be religious, and bridleth not his tongue, but deceiveth his own heart, this man's religion is in vain' (v. 26).

In verses 22–25 James was dealing with what we might call the foundation of the Christian's life—the need to come to the Word of God and to trust and obey the Christ who is revealed there. Those verses marry exactly into the parable Jesus told at the end of Matthew 7 about the man who built his house on the sand and the man who built his house on a rock. Jesus explained very clearly that the man who built on sand was a picture of a person who 'hears these words of mine, and does not do them' (Matthew 7:26 RSV) and that the man who built on rock was a picture of a person who 'hears these words of mine and does them' (Matthew 7:24 RSV). This is the point James has been pressing home in verses 22–25—the foundation of the Christian's life. Now he turns to the fabric of life, to the things that show on the surface, the outward expressions that prove —or disprove—the claim of an inner experience, and in this verse, he condemns false religion in three specific ways:

In the first place it is lacking in reality—'. . . seem to be religious . . . but deceiveth his own heart'. The picture here is of something that on the surface seems to be fine. It has the right name, the right shape, the right general appearance, but once you begin to examine it closely, you discover that that is all there is to it. It is lacking in reality. How penetratingly the Bible exposes that sort of thing! In 2 Timothy 3:5 Paul speaks of men 'having *a form* of godliness, but denying the power thereof' and the Lord's piercing analysis of the Church in Sardis was '. . . you have the name of being alive and you are dead' (Revelation 3:1 RSV). A form! A name! But nothing more!

Is that not true about so much of our Church life today? Even our evangelical church life? We have equated business with blessing, programme with progress, activity before men with acceptance before God, and I feel that so much of what we do as Christians is unreal, with no depth at all. The story is told of Arnold Thomas of Bristol being shown around St. Paul's Cathedral. During the tour he asked the guide whether he enjoyed his work. 'Yes,' he replied, 'But there is one drawback. I can never get to a place of worship!' I wonder if that is true in any respect in your life, especially in the sphere of 'religious observance'? Count up the number of hours you spend at it!—sitting in church, in prayer meetings, at Bible studies, at fellowship meetings, at rallies of one kind or another—but how often do you really get to a place of worship? The test of any act of worship is this—does it make us feel the presence of God? Joseph Twitchell tells how he went to visit Horace Bushnell when Bushnell was an old man. At night, Bushnell took him out for a walk on the hillside. As they walked in the dark, Bushnell suddenly said 'Let us kneel and pray.' Telling of it afterwards, Twitchell said 'I was afraid to stretch out my hand in the darkness in case I should touch God!' We have really experienced worship when we feel like that! Is much of your religion lacking in reality? Are you deceiving your own heart? Paul says 'For if anyone thinks he is something when he is nothing, he deceives himself' (Galatians 6:3 RSV), and the word 'think' used there is the same word in the original as the word 'seem' which James uses here. Here is the danger—assuming, thinking, taking it for granted that the form and the reality are one and the same.

In the second place, it is lacking in restraint—'. . . and bridleth not his tongue . . .'. This is the second thing wrong with the kind of religion James has in mind. It is lacking in restraint. We have a saying 'The truth will out', which means that sooner or later the real facts will emerge. Not only is that generally true, it is particularly true in the use of the tongue, which is why Jesus said '. . . out of the abundance of the heart the mouth speaks' (Matthew 12: 34 RSV). There can be a covering up for a certain time, but sooner or later—and in most cases I would guess it is sooner!—out of the mouth comes the truth of what is in the heart, and how often is it true that a tongue uncontrolled by the speaker is the mark of a heart uncontrolled by the Saviour. We must take this a little further. One of the most terrible things about sins of the tongue is that they come so *easily*. As Thomas Manton once said 'Censuring is a pleasing sin, extremely compliant with nature'. How true that is! Censuring, criticism, backbiting, bitterness, come so quickly to mind—and to mouth! We do not have to work hard to find fault in others. I am told that on some of the mountainsides surrounding the Norwegian fjords, the snow is sometimes so delicately poised that the sound of a human voice can bring it crashing down in an avalanche of damage, destruction and death. In just the same way there are situations and circumstances in our lives—at church, at home, in business— poised so delicately that the sound of a human voice—yours! mine!—can bring down an avalanche of distrust and disaster. How many times, even within our relatively closed Christian circles, a work for God has been blighted and frustrated by the effects of a carnal, uncontrolled tongue! It is no wonder that the Psalmist was careful to pray 'Set a watch, O Lord, before my mouth; keep the door of my lips' (Psalm 141: 3). False religion is so often lacking in restraint.

In the third place it is lacking in results—'. . . this man's religion is vain'. There seem to be two Greek words translated by the word 'vain' in the Authorized Version, and the exact meaning of the one used here is the one adapted as our heading to this section—void of result. Yet again, we discover here that the Bible is its own best illustrator, as we can see by reading part of the story of Paul and Barnabas a Lystra, as told in Acts 14. You will remember that as a result of the healing of a man crippled from birth, the people believed that 'The gods have come down to us in the likeness of men!' (v. 11 RSV). In the frenzy of excitement that followed, the priest of Jupiter tried to lead the crowd in worshipping the Apostles, but Paul restrained them, saying 'Men, why are you doing this? We also are men, of like nature with you, and bring you good news, that you should turn from these vain things to a living God . . .' (v. 15 RSV). Notice the point, and the use of the words 'vain things', which have the same root as our word 'vain' in James 1:26. Paul and Barnabas were insisting that in the matter of making a man right with God, the worship of these idols (or of themselves as men) was vain, empty, produced no result whatever. They could never produce, or in any way contribute to, the wonder of justification, a guilty sinner standing justified in the sight of a holy God. Now it is this definitive word that James uses in condemning false religion. He says that in the matter of a man's walk with God, superficial activity that is marked in the ways we have noticed in this verse is 'vain', it can have no results. Void of benefit and blessing. Let us underline that in two ways:

(1) *It means nothing to himself*. The man himself will get nothing from that kind of religion. There may be a lot of activity in it, but no advance, and there is a great deal of difference between the two. Beware of being involved in a religious roundabout—a life, a programme,

an orbit of organization that is always on the move but is never actually making any progress.

(2) *It means nothing to God*. To put it bluntly, that sort of thing cuts no ice as far as God is concerned. To the One who searches our hearts, superficial religious observance is a vanity. The Bible has a devastating indictment of this kind of thing—'Hear the word of the Lord, you rulers of Sodom! Give ear to the teaching of our God, you people of Gomorrah! What to me is the multitude of your sacrifices? says the Lord; I have had enough of the burnt offerings of rams and the fat of fed beasts; I do not delight in the blood of bulls, or of lambs, or of he-goats. When you come to appear before me, who requires of you this trampling of my courts? Bring no more vain offerings; incense is an abomination to me. New moon and sabbath and the calling of assemblies—I cannot endure iniquity and solemn assembly. Your new moons and your appointed feasts my soul hates; they have become a burden to me, I am weary of bearing them. When you spread forth your hands, I will hide my eyes from you; even though you make many prayers, I will not listen; your hands are full of blood' (Isaiah 1:10–15 RSV).

Let us face this serious truth together. Let us beware of 'vain offerings'. All of our outward religion and service that is merely superficial, anything that is characterized by self-interest or pride or a critical spirit; all of this is nothing more in God's sight than what the Apostle Paul in 1 Corinthians 3:12 calls 'wood, hay, stubble'. It is condemned by God in the here and now and will be consumed by fire in the there and then.

2. *True religion commended*—'Pure religion and undefiled before God and the Father is this, To visit the

fatherless and widows in their affliction, and to keep himself unspotted from the world' (v. 27).

In studying this verse, it will help us to begin with *two explanations*, and then go on to look at *two examples.*

Firstly, the two explanations.

(1) *This is not an opposite way.* James begins the verse with a very impressive introit—'Pure religion and undefiled before God (and) the Father . . .'. But how does he go on? Does he speak about some massive theological issue such as the deity of Christ, or redemption by the blood of Christ, or regeneration by the Holy Spirit? No!—he goes on straightway to speak about pastoral visitation and living a good life! Now is this a flaw in James's writing, and therefore in the unity and authority of Scripture? Is this an *opposite* way of salvation to the way spoken of elsewhere, and especially in the writings of the Apostle Paul who says '. . . by grace are ye saved through faith; and that not of yourselves: it is the gift of God: Not of works lest any man should boast'? (Ephesians 2:8–9). The plain and simple answer to all those questions is 'No, it is not an opposite way'. The issue of the alleged conflict between Paul and James really comes to a head in chapter 2 of James's Epistle, rather than in his first chapter, but this verse does raise the issue, if only by implication. Without taking time or space here to call the evidence, let me just crystallize the truth of the issue like this: what Paul is saying in verses like the one I have quoted from Ephesians is that *justification never results from good works.* What James is saying, over and over again, is that *justification always results in good works*, that good works are the natural outcome of a spiritual income! And of course if you read Paul and James widely and deeply

enough, you will discover that they also teach each other's distinctive truths—and that because they were both taught by the same Holy Spirit. So this is *not an opposite way.*

(2) *It is not the only way.* The two words 'is this' are expanded by J. B. Phillips to read 'will show itself by such things as', and this helps us to see exactly what James means here. He is not saying that what follows is the *only* action of which God approves, the *only* thing that can be classified as 'pure religion and undefiled'. What he is saying is that this is just a typical example of the way in which a living faith will express itself, the kind of thing you would expect to see in the life of a Christian.

Those, then, are two important explanations we need to bear in mind as we turn to the main body of the verse—this is not an opposite way; this is not the only way.

Secondly, the two examples.

(1) *Practical helpfulness*—'To visit the fatherless and widows in their affliction'. How utterly down to earth!—and yet how completely in tune with the rest of Scripture! A few moments ago we were reading Isaiah 1:10–15 as a solemn commentary on James 1:26—false religion condemned. If we now read on in Isaiah 1 we discover that they in turn are a commentary on James 1:27—true religion commended! 'Wash yourselves; make yourselves clean; remove the evil of your doings from before my eyes; cease to do evil, learn to do good; seek justice, correct oppression; defend the fatherless, plead for the widow' (Isaiah 1:16–17 RSV). Notice how precisely these words agree with what James is saying here! In Psalm 68:5 we read '. . . a Father of the fatherless and a judge (The Amplified Bible "protector") of the widows is God in His holy habitation'. What greater assurance

could we have that practical helpfulness is something that is near to God's own heart! Before passing on, we ought to notice that James's word 'affliction' also appears in the Authorized Version in many other forms; for instance, 'anguish', 'burdened', 'distress', 'persecution', 'tribulation', and 'trouble'. The main sense of the word seems to be 'pressure'. Does that open your eyes to the tremendous range of human need there is in the world today? There are people in your area, your city, your town, your village, your street, maybe even next door, who are under pressure of one kind or another. There is the pressure of a large family, or the pressure of inadequate housing conditions, or the pressure of a low income, or the pressure of chronic illness, or the pressure of unemployment, or the pressure of misunderstanding, or the pressure of unkind discrimination, or the pressure of a fractured relationship within the family. Pressure! Now James says that true religion will show itself in this kind of situation by the Christian identifying himself with people's need, and doing so in terms of practical helpfulness. Think of those pressures again, those near at hand. Is there something—or something else?—or something more?—that you ought to be doing? It may be something that costs—but it will be something that counts!

(2) *Personal holiness*—'and to keep himself unspotted from the world'. When James uses the phrase 'to keep himself' he is *not* saying that a Christian does not need God's help in order to live a godly life. He is not suggesting that while salvation is entirely a work of God's grace, sanctification is entirely a matter of man's effort. An enquirer sometimes tells me that he hesitates about becoming a Christian because he could not 'keep it up'. He has a high opinion of the moral demands of Christianity,

and an acute sense of his own inability to measure up to them. When a person says this to me, I always hasten to agree with him! No Christian can 'keep it up' on his own. He has moral responsibilities of course, which only he can fulfil, but this needs to be balanced by the truth that a Christian is '. . . kept by the power of God . . .' (1 Peter 1:5). This balance of truth is even more closely seen in Jude's little Epistle. In verse 21 he urges his readers to 'Keep yourselves in the love of God', yet a moment later, in verse 24, he commits them to the care of their God and Saviour who is 'able to keep you from falling'. Now there is the balance. 'Keep yourselves'—'(He) is able to keep you'. This is what we could call one of the mysteries of grace, and grace is always a mystery to man's mind because it is foreign to his nature. However impossible it might be to see it clearly in human terms, we must accept the clear teaching of Scripture. A Christian's progress, a man's walk with God, his developing maturity is not a question of God doing His part exclusively and without reference to man, and man doing his part exclusively and without reference to God, and the two coming together to produce the finished product, a mature saint. That is *not* the picture. What we see in Scripture is a balance, a balance which on the one hand teaches in the words of Harriet Auber's hymn,

'. . . every virtue we possess
And every victory won,
And every thought of holiness
Are His alone'.

and yet which still maintains that man is entirely responsible before God for his moral obedience. Of course in human terms that is impossible, and that is why I have called it a mystery of grace. It is all God's work, and yet it is entirely our responsibility. The Apostle Peter says '. . . brethren, give diligence to make your calling and election sure' (2 Peter 1:10). Now surely our calling and election can *only* be God's work. We can hardly claim a share in bringing about either of those! Yet Peter says we are to give diligence to make them sure—by prayer, by our attention to God's Word, by our obedience to the voice of the Holy Spirit, to prove their reality in our lives. This, then, is James's burden, that the Christian should do all in his power to 'keep himself . . .'.

The last phrase in the verse is 'unspotted from the world'. There are no details given, because all the world's spots and stains are included! All worldliness is forbidden for the Christian. Later on in the Epistle James goes so far as to say that '. . . the friendship of the world is enmity with God' and that 'whosoever therefore will be a friend of the world is the enemy of God' (James 4:4). What is worldliness? It is not so much a way of life as an attitude to all the circumstances and 'things' that go to make up life. It is the attitude that puts 'the things on the earth' before 'the things which are above' (Colossians 3:1–2). In *The New Bible Dictionary*, Professor R. V. G. Tasker says 'Worldliness is the enthronement of something other than God as the supreme object of man's interests and affections' and that is really the acid test. Listen to the Apostle Paul in 2 Corinthians 4:18—'. . . the things which are seen are temporal; but the things which are not seen are eternal'. What are the things that we can see? or weigh? or measure? or feel? or touch? or count? These things, says the Bible, are just temporal, passing. But how much of our mind and our time do they occupy? And how much of our interest? And how much of our care and concern are given to these things? Even more searching, how much of our devotion is given to them? Personal holiness is true Christian separation; separation *from* the world, and separation *unto* God. Part of a 17th Century hymn by Antoinette Bourignon, translated by John Wesley, puts just the right words to the resolve that ought to be ours. Make them *your* prayer—now!

> *'Henceforth may no profane delight*
> *Divide this consecrated soul,*
> *Possess it Thou who hast the right*
> *As Lord and Master of the whole'.*